History and Fiction

History and Fiction

Writers, their Research, Worlds and Stories

Gillian Polack

PETER LANG

Oxford • Bern • Berlin • Bruxelles • New York • Wien

Bibliographic information published by Die Deutsche Nationalbibliothek.
Die Deutsche Nationalbibliothek lists this publication in the Deutsche National-
bibliografie; detailed bibliographic data is available on the Internet at
http://dnb.d-nb.de.

A catalogue record for this book is available from the British Library.

A CIP catalog record for this book has been applied for at the Library of Congress.

This is the paperback edition of *History and Fiction: Writers, their Research, Worlds and Stories*, 2016, ISBN 978-3-0343-1981-2 by the same author.

This paperback edition first published in 2020.

Cover image: Photograph © Katrin Kania. The medieval manuscript pictured is Arundel 74 f. 2v from the British Library.

ISBN 978-1-80079-088-9 (print)   ISBN 978-1-80079-090-2 (ePub)
ISBN 978-1-80079-089-6 (eBook)   ISBN 978-1-80079-091-9 (Mobi)

© Peter Lang AG 2020
Published by Peter Lang Ltd, International Academic Publishers,
52 St Giles, Oxford, OX1 3LU, United Kingdom
oxford@peterlang.com, www.peterlang.com

This publication has been peer reviewed.

To Van Ikin,
an extraordinary mentor, amazing editor and very patient person

Contents

CHAPTER 7

CHAPTER 8

CHAPTER 9

Foreword

We all know that the past is dead and gone ... just as we all know that the past lives on everyday. We all accept that the past is unreachable and cannot be revived ... just as we all accept that the past shapes our lives every day. In short, we live with paradox around issues like history and the past.

Writers of fiction leap boldly into the midst of that paradox. They exploit it for commercial gain, they mine it for the magic it can be used to create, and on many occasions they explore it for the sake of the insights and revelations it can offer. *History and Fiction: Writers, their Research, Worlds and Stories* is Gillian Polack's ambitious and illuminating investigation of the role of the fiction writer in exploring history, creating new interpretations and reconsidering old ones.

In the period 2004 to 2010, and again in 2015, Gillian Polack conducted an extensive series of probing in-depth interviews with writers of historical fiction and speculative fiction. In total, around thirty writers were involved – an impressively wide sampling which included published novelists, short story writers, writers who were also publishers or editors, and specialists in historical fiction, historical romance, and historical fantasy. These interviews lie at the heart of this book and are an important and unique feature because they allow the practitioners to speak for themselves. The writers use their own working terminology, they offer their own perspectives on matters ranging from research to plotting to marketing, and they speak from their own personal professional experiences. Their voices are refreshingly honest and candid – you won't have to read for many pages to discover that! – and this down-to-earth pragmatism is both engagingly reassuring and illuminating.

I said the interviews are the heart of the book, but on reflection that's not the whole truth. The living beating heart of this book is Gillian Polack herself, with her extensive knowledge of this field. If I seem to be suggesting that this is a book with two hearts, that may not be as inappropriate as it appears. Gillian Polack holds two doctorates (one in History, one in

Creative Writing), and her life has two experiential cores (the theoretical concerns of the working academic and the praxis-based concerns of the working fiction writer). One of the things that delights me about this book is the way it combines dualities in every respect: Gillian's natural-speaking prose style effortlessly modulates into formal referenced academic discourse, and academic concerns about the ethics of historical appropriation sit comfortably against the writers' workaday focus on creating a compelling story.

Gillian Polack's experience in writing her 2014 historical novel, *Langue[dot]doc 1305*, has contributed to the depth of understanding that underpins *History and Fiction*. A work of speculative fiction, the novel involves a team of scientists who undertake a ground-breaking on-site research project by time-travelling back to St-Guilhem-le-Désert in 1305. Naturally, this story involved considerable historical research, as Gillian explains:

> I built up an image in my mind of the world of the Languedoc in 1305 using a mixture of primary and secondary sources, studies of social behaviour and mentalities, topographical and geological maps and a careful exploration of the region itself.

That sounds like the natural approach to the task, but – as *History and Fiction* will demonstrate – the writer's main allegiance is toward the telling of a good story, and the task is not a simple matter of joining up the historical dots. Sometimes dots have to be skipped over; sometimes they may even have to be invented. Those who deal in history and the past must learn to live with paradox ...

And they do, in their highly individual ways. Elizabeth Chadwick's fiction about twelfth-century England tends to focus on well-known and highly researched figures such as Elizabeth of Aquitaine and her family; Michael Barry is mainly interested in the dramatic 'grubby stuff' pertaining to historical figures; but Dave Luckett is wary of 'the pre-formed narratives of the famous'. Wendy Dunn celebrates the unknowable aspect of history ('what happens behind closed doors') because 'it frees us [writers] to be creators'; Kathleen Cunningham Guler strenuously seeks to avoid inventing history (but readily concedes that she has, 'both knowingly and unwittingly'); and Felicity Pulman describes her use of history as part of 'an intuitive, unconscious sort of process' whereby ideas for the story lead to research, and the research suggests other story possibilities which in turn require more research.

Similar sorts of alternatives and choices confront the team of time-traveller scientists back in Languedoc. They know they must not interfere with the past and must at all times remain impartial and objective in attitude – but that's easier said than done when it's your boots on that ancient ground. Just as the scientists have to negotiate potential conflicts and dilemmas, so the writers who use history in their fictions must shrewdly mediate between the expectations of readers and the findings of historians, and negotiate the demands of story against the factualities of dates and events.

History and Fiction provides a thorough and clear overview of these issues. Impressively, it does this from multiple perspectives, offering an overview that should please scholars but at the same time be useful for practicing writers ... and on top of that it should also prove illuminating for discerning general readers who want behind-the-scenes insight into the construction of the fictions they so greatly enjoy.

Allow me to conclude with Gillian Polack's own words:

> Novels allow us to feel as if we are participants in [the] past, bringing it to life and allowing us to play with it, to construct narratives that bring it to life. History is the way we mediate with that unreachable past and novels are a powerful way of mediating with that history.

Van Ikin
University of Western Australia
October 2015

Acknowledgements

This project has been a long time in the making. Without communities of writers and of scholars it could not have happened at all. Thanks to my group of science fiction, fantasy fiction and historical fiction friends for listening and arguing and helping me turn my questions into concrete understanding. Thanks especially to Melbourne science fiction fans for always asking 'Where are you up to?' and saying 'We want to know what's happening!', to the Historical Novel Society of Australia for their excitement about the project, and to all the students who pushed me that much further in my understanding through keeping me grounded.

Special thanks to the ACT Government for a research grant from ArtsACT, and to Van Ikin for shepherding me through the very difficult final legs. It's much easier to do a project over three years than over eleven, with other major projects interfering and one's own novels crying for attention. Van's encouragement, guidance and advice were invaluable.

There are thirty writers to whom I owe a particular debt of gratitude. Their generosity in revealing how they work and discussing their processes and thoughts so very openly was what made this study possible. Their work is discussed and they are the very best of colleagues and, in some instances, also the very best of friends. These people too, have cheered me on. I hope the results are useful! There are many other writers, scholars and friends who have given this study gentle pushes, including Lucy Sussex, Janeen Webb, Jack Dann, Sharyn Lilley, Stephanie Trigg, Helen Young, Joyce Chng, Rachel Kerr, Naomi Gambetta, Elizabeth Chadwick, Pamela Freedman, Mary Victoria, Valerie Johnson, Andrew Lynch, Kari Maund, Milena Benini, Sari Polvinen, Kathleen Neal, Julie Hofmann, Shana Worthen, Sam Faulkner, Kate Elliott, Richard Lagarto, Valerie Parv, Glenda Larke, Susan Bartholomew, Ambelin Kwaymullina, Edward James, Talie Helene, Kyla Ward, Lee Harris, Kate Forsyth and Jenny Blackford. Thank you all.

And to Dr Stuart Barrow, for checking the final, may I worship at your feet? My right eye went temporarily blind in the last few months of this book and I would not have been able to turn in a clean copy without his patience and attention to detail. I lost my sight in Sydney, on the day of a workshop, and I owe a lot to friends who shepherded me through the following weeks and to specialists who were patient with my impatience.

Thanks also to Sonya Oberman, for helping in a number of ways.

Introduction

Novelists achieve a different understanding of history to historians. Asking 'What is the relationship of fiction writers with history?' opens the door to many insights into the nature of creation and of narrative. It illuminates what history does in fiction and why some novelists take their historical research very seriously indeed.

This book explores the nature of the author's relationship with history and with their sources, from the author's own view and often using the author's own words, and it places the writer's relationship with history inside the wider perspective of how a novel is developed and the processes the writer must engage with to turn history into publishable story.

This volume is not about the past: it concerns fictions and tales and interpretation; it is concerned with the aesthetic. John Tosh's analysis (2006: 12) that popular historical knowledge 'is only incidentally concerned to understand the past on its own terms' applies. While writers appear to offer readers insights into how to see the past and play a role as educators on the meaning of history, in letting us feel as if we are participants in that history they are acting primarily aesthetically.

The terminology used in this work is heavily influenced by the terminology used by the writers being studied. It focuses on the concepts writers themselves use to articulate their understanding of history and how it relates to their work and to place it in a wider cultural framework.

Through the study it was apparent that, for the majority of writers, their work and their approaches to their work are intensely personal. The core of the research is a set of interviews with authors. The respondents cover a cross section of the publishing industry.

Three positions inform this book. The first is that of a historian, for I am one. The second is that of a novelist who uses history in her fiction, for I am one of those, also. The third is that parlous stance brought about by direct research into the writing habits of others, partly from an analysis of fiction and partly from interviews with a group of writers.

History as historians write is dynamic: knowledge and understanding are ever-changing and perpetually compared and contrasted with the knowledge and interpretation of other historians. The world for a writer is usually far more static. Why is this so? How does the writer navigate the dynamic and transform it into a novel? This book will identify and discuss key questions concerning why and how we use history in fiction and answer those questions using two key sources: the writers' own words as they talk about history and about their work, and the novels themselves.

The function that history serves in a writer's work has a strong bearing on what will be the most appropriate techniques for that writer to use, and the quality of the work within its own genre often depends on an appropriate choice of techniques. The techniques the writer deploys therefore have an important relationship with both the strength of the narrative overall and with the validation of the history within the tale.

There is a quantifiable difference between the research awareness of historical fiction writers and of speculative fiction writers within the group of writers interviewed. In some cases, this might be because the work of the historian does not provide the material needed by the fiction writer. In others it might be the style in which the novel is written, for some styles require more detailed information than others in order to interpret history effectively for readers. In most cases, however, writers did not articulate their relationship with the sources they used in the same way as a historian. Some writers work alongside scholarly history; some writers use their understanding of history as a springboard to create new worlds or to defend their personal truths. None of them write like historians; many of them do not write like each other.

At the heart of the choices writers make about the history they use in their fiction and how they choose to use it rest some fundamental historiographical questions. Why does history matter to them? What is it that drives writers to fictionalize the past?

Chapter 1 will examine how new approaches to historical narratives help us understand how writers explore the past, and how the work of fiction writers relates to modern historical study. Some of the chief purposes that history serves in fiction, and why writers use history, will be explored.

When writers think about a particular period in history, they contemplate a mediated set of narratives about places and times that are unachievable. Novels rely on specifics to communicate atmosphere, plot and character: specific places, specific people, specific events. Writers create fiction from narratives they know. When fiction writers bring a strong sense of history into their stories, they draw from the narratives of others. No writer works without these influences, even if they believe they do. No artefact lacks cultural contexts: writers are as capable as others of being influenced without acknowledging or even noticing this influence. This is one of the reasons the narratives of historians are – as a rule – problematic for most fiction writers.

One of history's roles is to interpret the past for others, to explain how we understand it from a reading of sources or a detailed analysis of available data or accumulated knowledge. It validates culture and creates paths to identity. The role of the fiction writer in exploring history, in creating new interpretations and in exploring old ones, cannot be underestimated. History is the way we mediate with that unreachable past and novels are a powerful way of mediating with that history.

Novels depend on a type of built world that relates directly to the style of the specific novel, with genre playing a significant role in what choices a writer makes. In contemporary novels, that world is similar to ours. For novels that have historical settings, the world built is intended to be historical in nature.

Some of the credibility of the built world relies on formal research. This work examines the methods by which writers build their historical world for the novel and the importance of the depth of the world building and the understanding that accompanies it.

Novels are not neutral creations, therefore, they are very dynamic forces within the cultures in which they operate. This will be examined more closely in Chapter 2, which will explore the reasons writers give for their work. When these reasons are examined, novels can be seen to play a different role to history, for the most part. The different role is related to the nature of the novel.

Not all world building has realism as its basis. Not all history in fiction is representative of possible or even credible realities. What convincing novels share, therefore, is not necessarily cutting-edge historical scholarship. They share the writer's emotional comprehension of the history that underpins the world of the novel.

Writers have a range of choices to make when considering how to apply history to their fiction. The outcomes of these choices vary considerably. For the reader, the credibility of those choices is of considerable importance if the writer is to be convincing in their use of history. Chapter 3 will also explore how writers increase the credibility of the history within their novels. From a historian's point of view, these narratives can be divided into those that are probable or are improbable. Assessing these divisions entails a discussion of what is credible: how this continuum ranging from probable to improbable appears to the reader.

These elements of culture are transmitted in a quite specific way. The writers studied were not 'writing novels', they were *writing specific novels* most of which could be labelled clearly as belonging to a particular genre. Writers themselves labelled the works. They describe themselves as writing historical fiction, for example, or historical fantasy.

A critical writing technique is examined in Chapter 4. This is world building, or the creation of the world of the novel. While the notion of world building derives from the world of speculative fiction novels, it is a critical technique for the writing of any fiction. Examining it elucidates critical differences in how historians and fiction writers use sources and the stages that a writer passes through in order to achieve an effective understanding of history for the purpose of writing a novel.

Writing techniques are only part of the story. More central to the ways in which history is incorporated in fiction is understanding the difference between the mechanisms of the historian's narrative and how they are different from that of the novelist. This will be examined in the first section of Chapter 5 in terms of four key factors: research, interpretation, responsibility and transparency. These are used within the creation of the world of the novel, whether it is perceived by the writer as historical, or whether it is an entirely created world based loosely on history.

There is a process of translation that happens. This translation is part of a complex process of world building and novel writing, and the way(s) the two operate for several specific authors will be examined, for it became clear in the process of undertaking this study that genre plays a critical part in this aspect of writing. The way in which writers see their world developing depends very much on how their processes interweave with their sense of what the audience requires.

Writing any novel that uses history in a substantial fashion requires the writer to work through a number of issues. Modern views of a period require some thought, for instance, or at the very least a reaction. Chapters 5 and 6 together examine why some authors decide to create a past that cannot be real and others choose to write their novel alongside a particular understanding of history. Genre is critical in writers' choices, but ethics also has a role. The critical role, however, is that of story: the needs of a particular style of story dominate how history is transmitted through fiction. The shape of the story the writer conceives is also the shape of the research the writer will call upon.

Chapter 7 looks more closely at the research decisions writers make and how they turn that research into the stuff of story. Chapter 8 looks into the role of story itself, and also how writers define four key terms such as 'truth', 'fiction', 'history' and 'historical accuracy'. While writers call on historical studies to develop the historical background in their fiction, the nature of the story determines how they use it. The function of history in a novel, therefore, is critical to how history is used. This function is closely linked both to genre and to a writer's understanding of what they intend to achieve with a work.

To work within genre and to interpret history into their fiction, writers use quite specific skills, which are discussed in Chapter 9 as a 'novelist's skills audit'. It is through use of these skills that the culture chosen is transmitted: specific techniques are used to bridge the gap between the sources (the history) and the reader. The choice of genre and the tools used to indicate genre are part of this, and linked to how the setting of the novel is communicated. The skills a writer uses for their writing are closely linked with how they see history and use it in their work.

The explanations writers give for creating their fiction further illuminates how history is approached and used by writers. What is strongly evident throughout is that the passion of the writer for history helps propel into the market the work they write using history: it is not a cold equation.

The past, history, historians and novelists

Writers create fiction from narratives they know. When they bring a strong sense of history into their stories, they draw from the narratives of others. These others may be historians, or they may be other writers (for writers are also readers of fiction), or other tellers of tales (through movies, cartoons, the visual arts). They may even draw directly from primary sources, explaining artefacts without the assistance of anything but their own background. This means, still, they bring narratives from that background, and that those narratives are not mediated by historians and generally do not acknowledge the influences of other cultures. No writer works without these influences, even if they believe they do. No artefact lacks cultural contexts: writers are as capable as others of being influenced without acknowledging or even noticing this influence.

To understand this more fully, we need to take two steps back. First, we need to understand current thinking concerning historical narratives, on the work of historians and how our cultures explain the past. But before we can do this, we need secondly to set up some basic definitions. What do we mean (in this context) by 'the past', by 'history'?

Terms such as 'history' and 'the past' and their relationship have been debated vigorously for many years. Two journals where the current state of this debate can be seen are *History and Theory* and *Rewriting History*. The relationship between these terms is fluid, because the terms themselves are fluid. This instability can be confusing so, within the confines of this volume, the definitions used by scholars such as Alun Munslow and Frank Ankersmit will operate: the past is not a narrative, but the temporal opposite to the future. The events in the past are gone. They are out of reach. They cannot be constructed in the exact shape they occurred. They cannot be revived.

The past can, however, be interpreted using artefacts and narratives. These narratives rely on theory and on philosophies, whether they are the ones that ground the Annales School of history (which focuses on everyday life and its extrapolation), or the higher end theory of scholars such as Michel Foucault (who made strong links between historical patterns of behaviour and current behaviour). The work of Emmanuel le Roy Ladurie, using Inquisition records and administrative documents to illuminate the daily lives of ordinary people in the region around Montaillou in France in the Late Middle Ages, illuminates the approach of the Annales School and also helps demonstrate how scholars can develop a complex and dynamic relationship with the past. This relationship creates history. It also creates the academic disciplines of history, archaeology, literary history and so forth. History is not only an academic discipline, with its own method and theory, but in its broader sense it is also an array of cultural narrative (as established by Hayden White, notably in *Metahistory* [1973]), drawing on popular or learned understandings of the past. Writers are integral to the development and maintenance of these cultural narratives.

When writers think about any period or place in history, they are really thinking about a mediated set of narratives about places and times that are unreachable. We cannot know what William I said to Taillefer on the march to Hastings. We can, however, reconstruct the possible route William took, the conditions of the march and, through contemporary references, the tale that Taillefer told the king (*The Song of Roland*) on that long march. We do this through the narrative go-between and reconstructions and analyses of the past that our culture provides: these reconstructions and analyses can take the form of histories and chronicles, but can also be popular (for instance, films and novels).

It is at this point that the writer of fiction enters the picture. They take what is historically 'known' (that is, interpreted) and they weave their own story (see Polack, 2008, for a fictional version of William's march to battle). Even if the fiction writer is also a historian, they still rely on the cultural understanding of the past and its various interpretations that other writers use. What this means for fiction will be explored by this book.

The role of the fiction writer in exploring history, in creating new interpretations and in exploring old ones, cannot be underestimated. Novels allow us to feel as if we are participants in that past, bringing it to life and allowing us to play with it, to construct narratives that bring it to life. History is the way we mediate with that unreachable past and novels are a powerful way of mediating with that history.

The value of fiction in communicating the past and of creating bridges between audience and formal history is high. One of history's roles is to interpret the past for others, to explain how we understand it from a reading of sources or a detailed analysis of available data or accumulated knowledge. It validates culture and creates paths to identity. Historians who work with this interpretation include John Tosh (see Tosh, 2006) and Greg Dening (see Griffiths, 2009).

How novelists do this through using history is by bringing readers into a narrative based on an invented world that rests upon their own interpretation of history. This is partly the role of the story, taking readers with it on a journey. Through introducing the reader to a new branch of a story or helping them see the story in a new way, the novelist can also expand the cultural validity of a construct. The marketplace plays a part in this, helping to validate the work of some writers over others and thus validating some new constructs and interpretations over others within modern culture. Through this, writers create personal bridges to a particular time and place. They provide the strong personal affiliation with a setting through their own intimacy with that setting (which is a part of writing a novel) and through how they present that intimacy to their readers.

All of these notions will be explored in more detail in their place. The key point that needs to be emphasized first, for it is the central element that brings everything together, is the importance of cultural validation. Fiction is not culturally neutral. It is not mindless. It fulfils a range of important socio-cultural functions, whether or not the writer intends it to. One of the key roles it fulfils is to validate culture, to enable people to attribute worth to their own experience and to provide narrative context for that experience. How this can operate within the field of science fiction is demonstrated by A. E. Levin (1977) who discusses the role conjectural literature plays in establishing – by developing a contrast with conjecture – an understanding of the experience and culture of the reader. An example of this is might be the failure of the rule of law in George R. R. Martin's Westeros, leading to an appreciation of the role of law in maintaining a stable society and thus validating the rule of law in modern Western countries.

The function that this study will return to over and again is cultural validation: the validation of culture through presenting truth, through recreating the past, through sharing a known story, and through offering the sense of a particular past as being part of the reader's culture and of that culture being shared. Thinking of the example of Martin's Westeros, it is not simply a matter of current rule of law being validated through history in fiction, it is the development and change of law over time: it is the history of the rule of law that we now experience that is validated and its changing roles interpreted.

In this, novels do not stand alone: the interpretation and understanding is not created by one author, but by a range of authors presenting the fictional history of a place. Each author, in their unique creation, interprets culture and history and plays a role in cultural validation.

Other purposes that history fulfils for the fiction writer will also be explored, including the roles authors feel their fiction fulfils in addition to telling a story well. Emotive connections between authors and history are particularly important.

All of these, however, are tools that lead to cultural validation or elucidate the role the particular fictional narrative plays in cultural validation. There are many approaches to this and many ways of examining cultural validation. For instance, Justine Larbalestier and Marleen S. Barr have looked closely at the roles of women in science fiction, and Camille Bacon-Smith has examined women as science fiction fans.

How does fiction do all this? Fiction is an interpretative act. This takes us back to the relationship between 'the past' and 'history'. All historical narratives interpret; they find for us ways of understanding, they discover that inaccessible past for us. Where non-fiction historical narratives differ from the novel are in the choices made by the historian as part of this interpretation. To educate, inform, to evaluate and present evidence and theories: these things are more important to historians than entertaining and are some of the key points at which the historian differs from the novelist (see Polack, 2014). The fact is, however, that they share narrative. The vast majority of histories and novels have beginnings and middles and endings and have an author's voice and other traits of narrative. The similarities are as important as the differences.

We develop those views from so many places. One of these places is our sense of history. We develop that sense of history, again, from many places: one of them is our fiction. Fiction is one of the pillars that hold up our culture and helps us to develop a sense of who we are and where we belong.

What has just been described is the bird's-eye view, but this study is not of the bird's-eye view. It looks at a deep question that helps us understand that bird's-eye perspective: why is history so important to writers? Why do many writers see history as important to their fiction? What roles does it play? How does it all come together?

At the heart of this particular study is a series of lengthy interviews with historical fiction and speculative fiction (science fiction, fantasy and horror) writers from 2004 to 2010 and a set of much smaller interviews in 2015. In total, twenty-eight writers were interviewed and around forty additional writers were consulted verbally. These writers cover a cross section of the publishing industry. They include published novelists, short story writers who are turning to writing novels and writers who are yet to be published. I received replies from historical fiction specialists, historical romance specialists, and historical fantasy specialists. A complete list of the writers directly used or consulted in this study has been incorporated into the index.

The results of these interviews (first reported in Polack, 2005) have been combined with other research to develop a close understanding of what writers do, what they think they do, and how they undertake it. The aim of the interviews was to discover some of the current views that writers hold about their own relationship to history. The common factors in the initial group of writers were that they wrote fiction (most wrote long fiction, that is to say, novels, but a small group wrote mainly short stories) and that they had an interest in the Middle Ages. The questions assumed an interest in the Middle Ages, rather than in 'history': this focus was intended to elicit more precise answers and a stronger awareness of their own work, but it also begs the question of whether writers address other periods in the same way. This question will be tackled throughout this study, through adding the work and views of other writers into the mix.

One of the most important questions the writers had to answer was why they use history in their fiction at all.

Chaz Brenchley, a US-based British writer of genre novels (ranging from mystery to high fantasy) explains his choice to use history in fiction:

> Like most of my career-shifts, this just happened to me. Specifically, meeting Tolkien had ruined my writing life: I'd always wanted to write fantasy, but I spent my teenage writing bad Tolkien and then swore one of those great adolescent oaths that I would write no more fantasy until I had an original idea. Twenty years later, the postman delivered it, in the form of a brochure advertising a reprint of Stephen Runciman's history of the Crusades. People in exile from their own culture, at war on all their borders, at war between themselves, magic and mysticism and myth all around them – if anyone had said 'Chaz, you should write a historical fantasy, with lots of research in it' I would have run a mile, but this felt ... giftwrapped.

Ross Hamilton – an Australian short story writer – expressed something similar. His main interest is writing speculative fiction and he said, 'I need plausible world settings.' He did however, have an emotive reason that influenced him towards using the Middle Ages, that is, he was not approaching his work from a purely pragmatic angle. He gave no explanation for the emotive side, however, but simply said, 'for some reason I am particularly fascinated by the medieval settings'.

Perth writer of speculative fiction (both serious and comic) Dave Luckett is another writer who uses the Middle Ages for pragmatic artistic reasons. He points out that 'the setting is a marker for a recognisable genre, and that in turn allows me to work with a set of conventions and reader expectations'. He can then work with those expectations or subvert them: they are a springboard for his craft, in other words. He also points out that he uses the Middle Ages 'because I know the period, not only its events, but the basic economic facts and society against which those events take place.' This reflects his own undergraduate training in medieval history.

Sally Odgers, a writer mainly of work for children, both historical and speculative fiction, also uses the Middle Ages mainly for technical reasons. She says, 'I like to write fantasy, and, like fantasy, Middle Ages settings give young characters a better chance to move about. Modern times aren't easy on adventure writers.'

Chris Andrews, another Australian writer, expressed similar sentiments: his aim was a sword and sorcery type of novel, which he feels is suited to a medieval background.

Other writers use the Middle Ages because it is technically useful to their writing. Catherine Butler (a British writer, also writing as Charles Butler, mainly for children and young adults) needed several settings for a particular novel. She says that, for one of them, 'I chose the Middle Ages because I needed a pre-Reformation setting in which alchemy was a possible interest for an ingenious goldsmith. My man is obsessed by Roger Bacon, so it clearly had to postdate him, too.' It was therefore a logical deduction based on the needs of her plot.

The next (small) group of writers have a very intellectual interest in history or genre and writing, which is important in informing their choices.

British historical fiction writer Brian Wainwright declares that he has 'a very deep, broad and abiding interest in the Middle Ages – I can't really remember when I didn't have but I think it was certainly established by the time I was eleven. I wanted to know about every aspect of life in those times, and I also wanted "answers" that formal history cannot supply.' For him, fiction was a means of supplying those answers. This is essentially an emotive response to the past, but for Wainwright, it comes with a historian's set of questions and the fiction is his tool for expressing and responding to those questions.

Tamara Mazzei (questioned as a publisher who writes, rather than as published writer: the boundaries between different parts of the publishing world can be quite porous, so the fact that her views are similar to those of several dedicated writers helps us measure the way these views spill over into and are shared by the publishing community) uses the Middle Ages as a tool to explore ideas about the passage of time. She comments: 'I like historical fiction and *Sex and the City* has already been done, [so] I wanted to focus elsewhere.' Her fiction, therefore, is really an investigative process, and the focus is on people and time. She has demonstrated a strong interest in the Middle Ages elsewhere (her publishing house, Trivium Publishing, places articles on the Middle Ages on its website) and an even stronger interest in history in general (Trivium Publishing was a major sponsor of Women's History Month in Australia for three years). She states very clearly, however, that her main concern in her fiction is not the Middle Ages, but the narration of the passage of time, as in a family saga. This is a clear articulation of her writing priorities rather than a dismissal of a particular historical period. Thus her interests inform her choices rather than compel her to make them.

Like Mazzei, Franco-Australian fantasy author Sophie Masson does not have a simple response when asked about her use of the Middle Ages in fiction. She is very positive about the historical period and has a clear mental image of it in her mind. 'I love the Middle Ages because they're so full of fantastic stories, and peopled with such amazing and individualistic characters. I love the contrasts of the Middle Ages –the frankness, humour, passion, beauty and earthiness combined with spirituality, violence, craziness and chaos.'

It is not the only period she uses, however. In addition to the Middle Ages, Masson uses nineteenth- and twentieth-century history in her alternate Earth fantasy novels, including recent novels such as *Scarlet in the Snow* (2013) and *Moonlight and Ashes* (2012), which have as their basis European fairytales. In fact, she has strong interest in history in general and will use period and place to create the particular atmosphere she needs for a specific novel. For example, she based her novel *Forest of Dreams* (2001) on her understanding of the life of twelfth-century poet Marie de France.

Her interest in using the Middle Ages is very precise. She says that, 'I am particularly interested in the period from the twelfth century on, because it seems to me that much of what's made Western culture so great, rich and diverse came from that period – including the ancestor of fantasy, in the Romance!' It is the romantic and fantastic elements that inform her fiction. She makes a clear connection between the emotive links with the period and what can be duplicated from that in a novel, thus her response is a carefully balanced one, with technical writing realities tied in very clearly with a natural interest in the period.

While Sydney writer Felicity Pulman talks about specific reasons for choosing a medieval setting for her Shalott trilogy and for the Janna mysteries (all originally young adult novels; the Janna books have since been adapted for the adult market), the most important element of her reasons is the link between them. She points out that, for the Shalott trilogy 'the essential elements of my story (the love triangle between Lancelot, Guinevere and Arthur, Elaine of Astolat, and Mordred's birth and betrayal) are all medieval inventions and have no place in the more "authentic" portrayal of Arthur as a dark age warrior.'

The link was the research she had to undertake:

> Researching Geoffrey (and the various dedications in his *History*) led me to a wider research of his time, and to the civil war between Stephen and Matilda. The plot possibilities inherent in a country (and families) divided by civil war influenced my choice of time and setting for my new series, The Janna Mysteries. The characters in the Shalott trilogy were partly or wholly dictated by the characters already in Arthurian legend. In The Janna Mysteries I wanted to portray a young girl adrift in medieval society with only courage, a willingness to learn and a talent for healing to help her survive, to empower herself and to succeed in her quest.

In her case, therefore, it was simple causation: her mind needs to be in the right place for a set of ideas to open up for a novel. Whether her interest in the Middle Ages remains intellectual or develops into the passionately emotional is something that will then become apparent as the novel itself develops.

Maxine McArthur's Middle Ages, like Pulman's, sprang from intellectual curiosity and from being in the right place for the intellect to feed into the novel writing process. Like Butler, she was working on a particular novel: neither writer dedicates their writing career to the Middle Ages. McArthur, in fact, is generally known for writing space opera and hard science fiction, through her duology *Time Future* (2008) and *Time Past* (2009). The young adult fantasy – *Hashimori* – she describes here (unpublished at the time of writing) is quite a departure for her, and says a lot about how the intellectual environment can lead a writer into new fields. Historical settings do not come from a single source and are not always explored by the same kinds of writer. She explains that:

> *Hashimori* grew from an eight-weeks writer's residence in Yamaguchi prefecture, Japan, in a small farming community in the mountains. Near where I was staying is an amazing limestone plateau, riddled with holes and under which is one of the largest limestone grotto system in the world. What writer could resist such a setting? I also wanted to write a world in which the folk tales of the area were real, and an

earlier age seemed apposite for this. I wanted to avoid the sword-wielding samurai epic, however. One of the things that bothers me about history, as it is generally taught, is all the people who get left out. Obviously we know very little about the illiterate lower classes in early history, unless it's through the eyes of their 'masters'. But it seems unbalanced to leave them out. I suppose folk tales are a distorted way to look back on those 'invisible' people.

At the far end of the spectrum are the writers who, for emotive reasons, feel compelled to use the Middle Ages as their main and preferred setting. Sandra Worth (a Canadian-American author who specializes in fiction set during the Wars of the Roses) admits, almost reluctantly, that 'I didn't choose the Middle Ages; the Middle Ages chose me.' She attributes her use of the period to an emotional – almost romantic – interest in it, and one she cannot fully explain: 'I have been enthralled with that period since early childhood: knights in shining armor battling evil; lovely princesses waiting to be rescued; castles on the hill.' She has moved on from there to looking at what history teaches us about our own lives, but this is an afterword in her explanation of why she uses the Middle Ages. Essentially she is entranced with it still.

English writer Helen Hollick expresses a similar love for history as being the reason for writing using British historical settings (including Arthurian, Saxon and pirate adventure settings). Wendy Dunn, Australian author of Tudor historical fiction, agrees, though quietly, in stating, 'I have been drawn to the Tudor period since childhood.'

These two writers express a very important need to understate the emotional links to the past. The strength of those links come out in other aspects of the interviews and will be discussed elsewhere, however it is important now to note that external pressures attached to writing genre fiction may cause these aspects to be stated with caution. Genre writers often face a literary world that dismisses them no matter how successful or skilled they are as writers, and it is quite possible that this has produced the need to understate some of the perceived 'negatives' of genre writing, in this case the strong emotive link between the historical fiction writer and the history they write about.

This suspicion is reinforced by the comments of the most self-consciously literary of the writers in the group, Canadian academic Robyn

Starkey. She justifies her use of medieval settings technically, by talking in intellectual terms about her aims in writing: 'I think part of it is wanting to write about the difference between modern industrial society and a world which uses magic instead of technology. So I think medieval-type settings are interesting to highlight this contrast.'

She has no trouble with the emotive links, but she is also very clear that she is writing for a small audience and that she is not a professional writer. Since she derives her professional acclaim from other aspects of her life, and her writing is less (by her own definition) genre fiction, she does not have to modify her emotional attachment to the past.

Others state this emotional link more directly. For instance, Kathleen Cunningham Guler, a writer published mainly in the USA whose writing focuses on fifth-century Britain, says that:

> Historical themes have carried a fascination for me since I was very young. Perhaps this is a need to fulfil some grander idealism or heroics I see contained in them that I find missing in my own time. I have also spoken at length with many other historical fiction writers who have indicated a sense that they belonged to other time periods and places. Many have openly expressed the idea that they may have lived in another life, another incarnation, in those times and that is why they gravitate to the particular era and place. Whether or not this theory is true, I have also found myself gravitating towards certain eras and places, and these are what I have chosen to write about. In conjunction, my heritage – Welsh and Scottish – bears heavily in the subject matter of my writing.

Her description implies that she is not merely writing settings, or crafting a novel, but using the Middle Ages because this period is somehow intrinsic to who she is.

Debra Kemp, a US writer whose novels are Arthurian, would agree with this and expresses herself most strongly of all:

> I wasn't given a choice. Let me explain. I did not grow up wanting to be a writer. As a child, I had a long list of professions, but writing was not one of them. But history was always one of my favourite subjects. As was English. Then one evening I saw a movie that changed my life. Literally. The movie was *Camelot*. I went home in awe of the concept of the Round Table. And I wondered two things. What could I find in the library about Arthur and Camelot? (I was very young and naïve. Good thing I love to read!) I also wondered – what if King Arthur had a daughter? What would

she be like in her father's shadow? Lin, as a character, was conceived that very night. Of course she has evolved since then. And I have been researching ever since. About thirty years now. I oft times feel like Lin chose me to tell her story, and I consider it a great honour.

It is not just an emotive connection with the Middle Ages that caused Kemp to write with it as a setting; she has a very strong personal emotive link with her invented character in addition to the link with the period.

UK writer of historical novels and historical romances Elizabeth Chadwick combines the three groups of reasons. She uses the Middle Ages partly for reasons of writerly craft, partly because she enjoys the investigative elements of writing involved in creating something with an historical theme, and partly because of a passionate attachment to certain aspects of the past. In other words, she has her emotive reasons for using the Middle Ages, but she also has the investigatory slant, and, implicit in her emotive reasoning is a deep understanding of genre and its articulation. It is appropriate to end this section with her reasons for using the Middle Ages, since they combine the reasons of most of the other writers.

All of Chadwick's novels have medieval settings, yet she traces her interest to adventure and fancy dress, rather than to pure historicism. She says:

> From childhood I was destined to write adventure fiction. It was what excited my interest the most. If I didn't write historical, I would probably write fantasy. An enlightened history teacher used to have us act out bits of history in front of the blackboard after we'd done the obligatory writing stuff about the event (complete with bits from the dressing up box). I used to love acting in these little dramas, especially if I got to wear the cloak.

She talks about her interest in the Hero's Journey (modelled on the monomyth identified by Joseph Campbell), effectively summarizing her interest in narrative set in the Middle Ages as an interest in heroic narrative, which often links to medieval settings.

It is particularly important that, once she had established her fascination with the heroic and the adventurous, Chadwick then went to great lengths to research and to make settings authentic. Her aim with this was to add the sense of reality to her stories. In her words:

Again, like when you're a child and you build a tent under the table. To make it feel more like the jungle you nick the rubber plant and stick a furry monkey in the branches and borrow your dad's binoculars. The props and surroundings had to be right, so I started researching. The more I researched, the more interested I became and the deeper became my involvement in the period.

Thus she began her path as someone who wanted to experience and tell tales of a particular kind and the specific historical interest followed from this.

What is particularly revealing about the stories Chadwick tells about her childhood is that they demonstrate an intense emotive link with history. This link is most often and most passionately expressed by historical fiction writers.

This level of emotion is seldom expressed by writers of speculative fiction. Dave Luckett, for example, is a Western Australian science fiction and fantasy writer with a solid background in formal history. Even with clear evidence of a passion for historical understanding both his formal education and his personal interest in the Middle Ages (communicated to me verbally), Luckett does not use such strong language to describe the links between his fiction and history. This less forceful and more pragmatic language is typical of the speculative fiction writers. In other words, there is a genre divide: the nature of the emotive link changes according to the genre being written.

While the division between writers interviewed suggests this genre divide, the quantity of evidence available makes the conclusions here suggestive rather than solid. A greater range of genres would have to be factored in, for instance, to fully understand the role genre plays in this. However, the differences between the speculative fiction writers and the historical fiction writers were quite clear: it is quite possible that the writers' relationship with history pushes them to one genre over another.

This leads to a more basic question. Why do these writers choose to use history and historical references in their fiction at all? Why do they make this initial choice?

Elizabeth Chadwick, again, explains that whilst her link with history was primarily emotive, it also related to the underlying narratives that she associated with history. We have already seen her interest in adventure. She adds, however, that:

> I can trace my interest in medieval history back to such embryonic beginnings as
> the above. I was always fascinated by historical adventure films on the TV and I've
> always been a sucker for the Hero's Journey. When I started writing originally, I
> wanted to tell adventure tales like the films I'd seen – *The Vikings, The Warlord, The
> Black Shield of Falworth*. However I wanted my stories to seem as 'real' as possible.
> Again, like when you're a child and you build a tent under the table ... The more I
> researched, the more interested I became and the deeper became my involvement
> in the period.

Thus the emotive links and the need to explore narratives drew her towards
the Middle Ages and her involvement with the research element created
its own addictive strand.

Sandra Worth again explained that the Middle Ages gave her an emotional validation and an important path into exploration and understanding of humankind:

> I suppose a cagey answer would be that I didn't choose the Middle Ages; the Middle
> Ages chose me. [...] But I grew up I came to realize that history teaches us about
> ourselves: where we came from, what's important and why. Unless we look back and
> appreciate what others died to give us, we can't get a perspective on our own lives.
> One thing I've learned from my study of history is that mankind doesn't change.

Brian Wainwright, as we have seen, reflects Luckett's interest in the period,
and combines it with Chadwick's passion. He himself, however, can be quite
precise about where his interests lie without being able to explain why. It
is interesting that he directly admits this when he says:

> For some inexplicable reason my main focus of interest is 1385–1485; I am inter-
> ested in the earlier periods but I don't pretend to know so much, and indeed my
> knowledge tapers off so I know a lot more about Edward I than William the
> Conqueror or King Stephen. That makes it easiest to write about the 'Yorkist
> hundred years' (as I think about it) because it minimises (but does not exclude)
> the need for fresh research.

Robyn Starkey is informed by the narratives she reads. She, like Luckett,
has advanced training in the field, so it is interesting but not surprising
that she has a higher level of self-awareness and historical reflexivity than
most of the other writers. She explains that:

> I use historical themes because I like medievalist fantasy, so I think that informs what I do. I also use fairy tales, which are often medievalist as well. I think part of it is wanting to write about the difference between modern industrial society and a world which uses magic instead of technology. So I think medieval-type settings are interesting to highlight this contrast.

The emotive link is there, but is expressed with more awareness of the way history is explained by historians. Starkey overrides this awareness however with her last comment, 'I also really want to write an historical fiction book based on Caxton because he is such a fabulous character.'

As we have already seen, Butler favours history as a professional tool rather than as a path through the wilderness. Felicity Pulman is equally rational in her primary reasons for selecting the Middle Ages:

> I deliberately chose a medieval setting (in an alternate reality) [...]. My decision to incorporate 'real history' came later, after one novel stretched to three and I began to explore the character of Guinevere, her love for Lancelot and her need for a child. I liked the idea of creating a child to bring a letter into our world, thus introducing the legend of King Arthur to Geoffrey of Monmouth while providing an explanation of the 'mysterious document' he claimed inspired his 'History of the Kings of Britain'. [...] The series will chart Janna's journey as she comes to a true understanding of herself while learning the secrets of the past. The location of the series was dictated by the story itself: I needed a forest (Grovely Wood) and two abbeys (Wilton and Amesbury) and a farm, and they needed to be reasonably close to Winchester, site of the royal treasury. Sites involved in the civil war also influenced my choice.

In other words, the needs of the story came first for Pulman and the interest in the period and the narratives about it came later.

At the opposite end are writers for whom the history comes first. Sophie Masson, for instance, Debra Kemp or Wendy Dunn.

We are seeing the same pattern emerge here as we did earlier: the emotive link to history is claimed as a crucial reason for using history in fiction by some authors and less so in others and the choice roughly falls along genre lines.

Fantasy and romance writer Nicole R. Murphy writes quite different novels to those thus far discussed. She has the love of history expressed by historical fiction writers, but her narrative sources are all romantic and epic in nature:

> I use historical themes because I've always been a bit of a history nut, and I use the Middle Ages because I was brought up on *The Lord of the Rings* and Shannara, and it also fits the romantic aspect of what I write. I have been researching the Norman period in England as the era in which to set my work, mainly because the dates are quite clear (just look for 1066) and so it's easy to research and to know whether what you are reading is good enough for the time zone or not.

Murphy demonstrates, as Chadwick did, that the narratives of writers are heavily influenced by the narratives of other writers and what they think about history and how they write about history is shaped by this reading.

Writers' thoughts on their work do not stand alone; they work within the cultural and historiographical perspective that was discussed earlier. The problem with the enthusiasm for history demonstrated by fiction writers, whether it is prompted by a love of a period or a plot requirement, is that it rests on what we have remaining to us of the past. Culturally in this context, the Middle Ages is an interesting case. Surviving sources for the period are not unlimited and they need interpretation. Without that interpretation, or with limited or naïve interpretation, the story reads differently to the way it would read if it followed the narratives of historians very closely. While this will be discussed in depth later in the book, it is important to flag it now. Just because a writer cares about history does not mean they write history into their fiction with the same skills as a historian: other factors come into play. Fiction is a cultural narrative: it is never a neutral vehicle for information about the past.

***

It is not only sources and knowing how to use them that restrict the possibilities for fiction writers. Academic historical method itself often runs counter to writers' perceived needs (see Polack, 2014). This points to a fundamental difference in types of narrative and to the quite different requirements scholarly history has as compared with fictionalized history.

Historical method is primarily a tool for ethical focussed inquiry. The narrow use of sources and the demand for a precise set of carefully formulated question and answer in relation to those sources leads to a better understanding of that element of the past. The classic introductory discussion of this is Carr (1987), however John Tosh's work into the nature of historical inquiry has superseded many of its assumptions. Historical method is primarily a tool that provides an interpretative bridge *between the past and history* (again, the work of Tosh and Foucault are particularly useful in this regard). It is not, however, a bridge *between fiction writers and history*. Scholarly research produces tightly focussed results that may only be of limited use in narrative terms (which will be discussed later) but it also produces quite a different view of a society to that produced by research for fiction.

General overviews of periods by scholars bring together knowledge at a given moment, but that understanding can radically change within the history profession and the results may not reach the general public for a number of years. For instance, the overviews of the Middle Ages that are traditionally used as a basis for teaching its history are those by Marc Bloch and Georges Duby. These studies rely on medieval history being deeply grounded by a strictly (or very close to strict) feudal society. Susan Reynolds in *Fiefs and Vassals: the Medieval Evidence Reinterpreted* (1994) has successfully challenged the uniformity of feudalism and even its nature. A successful alternate overview, however, has not yet been fully developed and thus Bloch and Duby still provide the basis for the popular works about the Middle Ages that writers such as Ian Mortimer in his *The Time Travellers' Guide to Medieval England* (2008) create. These popular guides are often the first port of call for fiction writers seeking to develop their understanding of a time and place.

Moreover, where sources for a particular group are lacking, generalist historians themselves fall back on stereotypes or completely avoid addressing a subject. Monique Bourin (2005) is clear in articulating the current deficit in understanding of the Languedoc in the Middle Ages. Any writer wishing to write about this area has to rely on analyses of other regions from a similar period: this leads to inaccurate and even misleading history.

Historians' view of the historical record is not complete, in other words. It cannot fill all the holes writers want filled. It cannot fit all the holes historians want filled. One of the major discussions in modern scholarship about the Middle Ages, for example, is how to give voices to the silenced: to women, to children, to Jews, and how to explain medieval emotions and masculinities. Answering these questions will fill in gaps, but there will always be aspects of the historian's understanding of a place and time that are either not relevant to fiction writers or that do not meet their specific needs. There are different dreams of the past within any given culture.

The most important element of the difference between historian responses and fiction writer responses to history here is that the limitations of historical method and coverage influence writers' capacity to develop characters and place them in realistic settings. For instance, the particular lack of knowledge we have of women's work and roles in the fourteenth century posed a particular problem for Brian Wainwright when he tried to reconstruct Constance of York's private life for *Within the Fetterlock* (2004). He had his grand vision and then had to spend twelve years in research trying to fill in enough details to write the novel (verbal communication, August 2011). Most professional fiction writers do not have the luxury of intensive research lasting many years, but the bottom line is that not even twelve years of research gave Wainwright sufficient information and understanding. The problem was that there were insufficient studies relevant to his needs and quite possibly insufficient primary sources to inform future studies on the relevant subjects.

While historians of the Middle Ages such as Judith Bennett and Monica Green in their work on women before the law and women's health treatment are remedying some of these deficits, the situation for writing fiction about women and children in the Middle Ages is grim. Authors have to find other ways of convincing the reader that their narrative is trustworthy than being able to honestly say, 'I have researched this and the current research on this by scholars has all the information I require, therefore my account can be relied upon.'

While using extensive research and developing a better understanding of the explanations of historians can help writers, they cannot universally do so and other techniques for convincing readers about the credibility of each narrative become important. These other reasons will be discussed later.

While the work of historians can be critical to the work of fiction writers, providing the critical interface between them and their use of history, this is not an appropriate place for a formal disquisition on the current state of historiography. It is essential, however, to possess a certain understanding of that state to understand its relationship to writers who use history.

Jerome de Groot (2010: 25–6) says that Georg Lukács argued that history was process and that historical fiction was a way of demonstrating historicity, and that it communicates and educates through fiction. John Tosh and Sean Lang remind us that E.H. Carr's *What is History?* was about 'problems of historical inquiry' (2006: xi). Processes are the unifying element in historiography, not facts. Scholarly history is the search for an understanding (and what that understanding is, changes), whereas most fiction is not about that search, but about presenting the understanding ready-made.

Lukács recognizes that novelists such as Flaubert, Austen and Balzac can express deep complexities in their fiction (Malvasi and Jeffrey 2005: 30). These complexities, however, seldom address the same issues that historiography addresses. John Fowles successfully does so in *The French Lieutenant's Woman* (1971), but this novel – like other works that are highly conceptual in nature and of great literary merit – is unusual. While some novels of this level of sophistication will be used as examples in this book, this study will also discuss novels that are less significant in literary terms, for the role of history in fiction is not confined to works of genius.

The very specific nature of a character-based or politically oriented novel (such as those presented as standard historical fiction or historical romance) works alongside traditional historical narratives. Writers such as Elizabeth Chadwick and Sharon Kay Penman are able to use medieval narrative sources. For instance, Chadwick uses William Marshall's *vita* for the novels about Marshall, as she indicates in the author note for *The Greatest Knight* (2005). She also uses modern political history about the period (largely based on these same narrative sources) to create a framework in which the fictional elements of the narrative can clearly rest.

Not all fiction is as amenable to genre. The further the narrative moves from well-documented lives, for instance, the more difficult the narrative is to sustain and the further the tale moves from well-documented history (places, times, classes, occupations) the greater the gap between the traditional historian and the fiction writer.

Even when fiction writers and historians appear to be walking along the same path, there are significant differences. Robert Penn Warren points out that historians know about the past and want to find out about it, but that fiction writers need to climb inside (1969: 61). How writers of fiction climb inside the past will be discussed in more detail when we look at how they create the world of the novel.

The fact that the two paths can be quite different, even when they are underpinned by the same primary sources and the same understanding of the past is, however, exceptionally important. Both paths are concerned with producing cultural meaning. This, too, will be discussed later.

As we have already seen, some novelists readily admit that their work has an emotional driver. This is no less true of historians. History has multiple functions: it can be remembering, or interpreting the past, but it can also heal, speak truth to power, entertain, uncover. To distinguish between history and fiction one must think more about how the meaning is expressed than specifically what meaning is given to the narrative. Discussion in the 1980s and 1990s of this aspect of history helped describe history as a literary form (see Curthoys and Docker, 2010) and of historians as 'engaging in literary experimentation in imaginative and innovative ways'.

This enables us, now, to compare literary genres, including history as one of them (for this comparison and further explanation see Polack, 2014). The importance of this comparison is that it enables us to understand that fiction uses history in the same narrative culture as the history itself. This is why I refer to my own fiction on occasion in this study: it is to reinforce the important understanding that the division between scholarly narrators and fiction writers can, at times, be artificial and depend wholly on the nature of the narrative and how that narrative is perceived.

***

If there are borders between scholars and writers, then those borders may be crossed. The question is how easily these borders are crossed and in what conditions. This and the different views expressed by authors of different genres lead to a deeper question concerning the nature of historical fiction and fantasy: how precisely do writers of these genres use history, how do they understand it?

The role of research in this is part of a larger question, which is: *How much understanding of the world of the historian does the writer need? (Is it sufficient to say 'I love this period' or 'I need this period for this particular piece of work'?)*

This capacity to compare does not mean that there is an equal respect for each use of history. C. Van Woodward claimed that 'I find among novelists more respect for and awareness of good history than I find among historians a proper respect for and awareness of good novels' (1969: 50). There are different levels of appreciation and different levels of understanding in different groups of historians and in different groups of novelists, and those levels and the nature of that understanding is dynamic over time. The task of this work is to draw out some of the differences between writers, through focussing on genre writers, and to more fully understand why and how they develop an awareness of good history, when and why they don't, and just what the dynamics are within their writing and their communities.

Peopling a book or setting the scene and working the plot all generate historical needs. Some needs are deep (the mentalities of characters, their world view and responses to their environment, for example) and some are essential to main a sense of the period (these manifest as carefully described detail: the style of dress or armour, the table setting, how one takes tea, for instance). Different novels have different requirements, and the genre difference between historical fiction, historical fantasy, historical romance, science fiction with historical settings – part of the way the reader categorizes each of these books – can be perceived through the historical aspects the author uses. All of these aspects of a novel feed into the story.

***

What do fiction writers offer that comes less easily to historians? One answer to this is point-of-view. Historians usually have a static narrator (themselves) who operates in the limited realm of what can be known and how the sources can be used to inform or expand or interpret this. Narrators in fiction are far more flexible. They can indicate the unreliability of our understanding of the past, or suggest special insights. They can offer alternate points of view. This clarifies the relationship between the interest in the Middle Ages expressed by, for instance, Debra Kemp and her passion to tell one particular story: for her, Arthurian history is not something that belongs to a dry, third person narrator; she sees it as flowing from and around the character. The nature of the narrator in the novel changes according to the point-of-view needs of the writer.

There are some fundamental differences in the writing choices of novelists and historians. For instance, the problem of presenting a balanced view of history and retaining the contexts that explain that view is quite different for the novelist to the historian. Both choose to match the focus to the narrative, but the historian can write the general overview of a period or even a series of periods whereas the novelist (even in such grand narratives as Tolstoy's *War and Peace*) almost always has to take a fine focus and present individuals and their lives. Even the sweeping science fiction of Stephen Baxter moves from fine focus to fine focus in presenting millions of years of humanity. This is because, with fiction, the reader needs a way to identify and to personally interpret the novel, and the easiest way to create this link between reader and writer is through characters. Thus the fiction writer almost always has the need to create a level of focus that works for individual characters.

The reader always plays a critical role in this, even if a writer is not writing specifically for one reader. How historians write for readers is, alas, tangential to this study. Less tangential is what readers expect from their historical fiction. Fortunately, M.K. Tod's 2013 Historical Fiction Survey addresses the latter question, albeit cursorily. Tod established that readers sought quality of writing, but also a sense of immersion in time and place. Education, romance, universal themes were additional preferences expressed by female readers. Those readers for whom historical fiction accounted for more than 50 per cent of their reading listed the classic novel traits of a good dramatic arc (linked, however, to historical events), to characters, to the immersion and to the 'authentic and educational'. All of these, I feel, may be how the most important category of 'superb writing' can be broken into some of its component parts.

The significance of immersion is key to understanding historical fiction. The most important reason for choosing historical fiction given by readers surveyed by Tod concerned bringing the past to life, and particularly the lives of people. The story elements (reading novels because they were great stories) was also important, but fell considerably short of the 'bringing the past to life' in terms of popularity. Other reasons for reading historical novels simply added to the 'bringing the past to life' argument, for they include understanding and learning about the past, time travelling through reading and connecting with the past in one way or another. Education and entertainment are so close in readers' minds, that they cannot be separated: the learning and the entertainment are bonded. This fits well with how historical fiction writers perceive their work, as we will see later.

No equivalent questionnaire has been undertaken for readers of other types of novels that use history. Historical fiction's place on the spectrum of fictions that use history is, however, clearly at the conservative end and, as we will see, writers of historical fiction are close to their readers in their desire to present and immersive, accurate past. Tod's study serves, therefore, as a sea-anchor for this study.

CHAPTER 2

Balancing truth, drama and art

Writers have many reasons to create novels. These novels are influenced by a writer's education, their relationships with their readers, and their relationships with the publishing industry. All of these are potential causes for a writer to create a novel. They might be writing to explain material they feel the outside world needs to understand, as a way of communicating with readers, or to make a professional income within the publishing industry.

When asked a direct question about the underlying reasons for their writing, writers gave very clear explanations of why they do what they do. The aim of the question was to uncover some of the principles that underpinned their writing overall and the use of history in their fiction. Specifically, I asked the writers their views of the three principles delineated by William Rainbolt (*Writing History/Writing Fiction: A Virtual Conference*). He describes three things as applying to his writing:

1) The Runciman Desire, where the fiction writer introduces truths that cannot be proven historically
2) The Oates Gambit, which draws people into reading history through the drama of fictional narrative, and
3) The Ellison Mandate, which is whether or not the book succeeds artistically.

Authors were asked to comment on the three in terms of how each relates to their own writing, plus to add to them if there were other factors that were of importance.

The writers interviewed presented very mixed reactions to Rainbolt's conceptualization. For instance Elizabeth Chadwick suggested that 'All are fairly important I would say, but again they're born of instinct and not conscious thought on my part', while Sandra Worth explains that her approach is governed by 'Educating, entertaining, and perhaps even changing the reader so that he sees things differently at the end than when he started.'

Dave Luckett challenged the three outright:

> I'll take one and three as vital, and for the Oates I'll substitute the Heinlein Imperative, which is to estrange reality for the paradoxical purpose of making it comprehensible. I don't think people read historical fiction to learn anything about medieval society, or any other, specifically. I think they read it because it sneaks up on reality sideways. What reality? Why, their reality, of course. A 'historical' is different enough from what they know to offer a change in perspective. One can understand an object better if one looks at it from several angles, and often the most divergent angle gives the most insight. Hence, fantasy and science fiction, also: wider angles.

Brian Wainwright also presented a partial and not entirely wholehearted agreement with the categories:

> I suppose I can tick the Runciman Desire; I am not sufficiently pretentious to believe that my novels will fill people with a burning thirst for knowledge of history; nor do I seek to be a great artist – for me the book either works or it doesn't. If it's still being read and enjoyed in a hundred years then maybe, maybe, it will qualify as great art.
>
> I would add – it's simply another way of enjoying history. I don't see why history need be a dry academic subject, or a deadly serious examination of fact. There can be other sides to it. As well, not instead.

This statement accepts Rainbolt's trinity as a legitimate means of exploring the subject, for Wainwright is positioning his own writing within Rainbolt's structure quite comfortably.

Odgers also specifically places her work firmly in the context of the Rainbolt analysis:

> I almost never use the Oates Gambit. I try to keep to 'truth' and accuracy, but I never use history for the sake of teaching. My fiction is written to amuse and entertain, even when it's serious. I may use the Runciman Desire, by using 'best guess', and I certainly want my books to succeed artistically.

Catherine Butler's response is similar: 'Of course I want it to be a good book. But no, I have no didactic intent, certainly not of a historical nature'. Felicity Pulman is more tantalized by the categories:

The Runciman desire is an interesting concept; I've found that sometimes I make stuff up and later I find that it is true, e.g. At the end of *Shalott*, [the character] El gets the plague – very necessary in terms of plot to add suspense, but that thought didn't come until later, until after I'd puzzled over Tennyson's lines: 'For often through the silent nights, A funeral with plumes and with lights and music went to Camelot.' I wondered why there were so many deaths? The plague seemed a good explanation, even though it was far too late for my purposes. But I used it anyway, and then discovered later that various forms of the plague had occurred through the centuries, and I found a reference to plague coming to Gwynedd at about the time of the 'real' King Arthur. So one thing led to another and it all fitted neatly and there was a real 'truth' to it. Even if stuff isn't true (like Geoffrey of Monmouth receiving Guinevere's letter through Callie) if it sounds right *and it works* then I'm happy to incorporate it. I don't at all consider the Oates Gambit when writing my stories, while the Ellison Mandate begs the question: in whose opinion? In the first instance I write for myself, so it's only my opinion that counts. Once the editors get their hands on the manuscript ... But even so, I will only make the changes I'm comfortable with. I think Rainbolt might have missed something important which I suspect applies to all fiction writers, not only writers for children: the desire to explore and explain issues of concern to the writer, and in the writing perhaps also to lay aspects of the past to rest. For example, I see the same themes recurring in my novels. I don't set out consciously to explore issues of identity and so on in my books and yet, looking back on my childhood, I know why these concerns are important to me. And I think this leads to a passion and a truth in my story-telling which is why I write what I write and why I don't do something – anything – that's easier and pays better!

Australian speculative fiction writer Chris Andrews says: 'I write fiction – fictional characters in fictional situations which at best may be placed at a certain period in history ... I don't pretend to write anything but fiction.' Avoiding the question of what fiction is and what its purposes are, Andrews declares: 'Rainbolt's principles aren't something I would even consider'.

Sophie Masson and Wendy Dunn agree about the importance of the Rainbolt categories to their work, but Masson is at clearly the other end of the spectrum from Andrews, for she does not simply consider and accept Rainbolt's categories, but adds one of her own. 'These are all true,' Masson explains, 'but I would add also, getting to the "heart", the mindset of a period through historical fantasy has been immensely satisfying. I'm not interested in just depicting the mundanities of medieval life, but also its myths, the things people lived by.'

Kathleen Cunningham Guler explains clearly why some of Rainbolt's thoughts work for her fiction and some do not:

> I recognize the Runciman Desire and the Oates Gambit very much in my writing. The challenge of research is to not only learn as much as possible about a particular era in order to write a solid and fulfilling story, but also to understand the inner workings of the people and events involved in a way that perhaps no one else has thought of before. [...] All this goes hand in hand with getting people to enjoy and appreciate history. If they feel they have learned something new and interesting through a form of entertainment, then perhaps – and hopefully – their curiosity will carry them forward to study a bit on their own.

Chaz Brenchley is equally clear concerning what applies to his work and what does not:

> I don't think I care much about the Oates Gambit; it has never occurred to me that people might use my books as a direct channel to history, and I certainly don't think of that as any part of my job. (I will enthuse about books I read, but I think that's a different thing.) The Runciman Desire – well, yes. I do that all the time, it's at the core of my practice. And the Ellison Mandate would lie at the heart of my desire.

There is a moral in this story. The classification that works for one author to explain a set of issues does not always work for other authors. In fact, the surprize some of the interviewed writers expressed when faced with Rainbolt's three elements demonstrates clearly the difficulty of extrapolating from the work of the few to explain the work of the many. It is yet another instance when the individuality of each writer is as important as what they agree on. The importance of that individuality will appear more than once in this study.

One theme that occurs over and over in the discussion of Rainbolt's categories, however, is that all writers wish to create a good novel. It is important to examine the factors that writers are willing to consider as important in this regard. This will help contextualize the responses to Rainbolt's three categories. While the writers were asked about a specific list of factors that they took into account to create that good novel, they were also encouraged to add key factors that were missing from the given list. The suggested factors were:

- marketability (was England in the twelfth century perceived as more marketable than Spain in the seventeenth, for instance)
- what readers have indicated that they enjoyed about the writer's previous work
- the preferences of a particular publishing house or editor
- the views of a writers' circle or support group
- other fiction
- accessibility and quality of research materials.

Elizabeth Chadwick is not primarily concerned with marketability. 'I write what I personally want to write,' she explains. 'I'm fortunate in that readers want to read it! If ever I lost my publishing contract I might have to think of writing something else, but it would be just a job rather than a passion. I write contemporary short stories for women's magazines for bread and butter. I know I can do it, but it doesn't give me that same buzz as writing medieval fiction.'

Her readers actively communicate with her:

> Reader preferences when I receive letters are usually for historical accuracy, feel for the period, the sensual aspects (i.e. all the touchy feely sight, sound, smell stuff that makes them feel as if they're living in the Middle Ages with the characters. They also like the emotional dramas that are played out and are very fond of the love scenes!!!). I take note of all these, but as the above is basically just the way I write, it's mostly a case of not being broke so don't fix it.

She is not at all influenced by writers' circles or other novels and is very practical about research sources, saying, 'Bummer if they're not readily available but it hasn't put me off so far'. Despite this comment, the research she does is significant and also quite critical to her work and will be explored in more detail in its place, as will that of the other writers.

For Sandra Worth, likewise, marketability is not a major factor: 'I had to write what I was driven to write, without regard to its marketability. That proved an enormous obstacle once I reached the publisher stage, since market is everything to them.' Her approach, however, resonates with her readers, who comment favourably:

... that I made history come alive for them. 'A history lesson to take to heart.' They cared about my historical figures, and related to them. One reader even said she thought about how Richard might have handled a situation she came to encounter in her own life. Many readers have told me that they come away from the book with a renewed appreciation for living in modern times – with our legal protections, our freedoms, and our ease.

Worth puts her finger on something that affects other writers. 'New York loved my writing and my books, but "historical fiction doesn't sell". They didn't expect the book to be published because it was historical fiction. When the book won a major award and was picked up by a publisher, I no longer received notifications to attend the meetings.' When writers and readers meet in their needs, marketing the book to reach the readers is not without issues: the publishing industry and writer circles are not always aware of this alignment between reader and writer interests.

Research is an interesting factor in Worth's list. Research

has proved difficult for me in Texas, but since my husband travels a great deal on business, I have been able to visit libraries across the country from Stanford to Harvard, as well as England, where I had a pass to the British Library's Manuscript Room for five years while researching Richard III, and I made more than three Ricardian trips to England during the period I was writing about him. Nevertheless, it's not like you can plan a day trip to the castle you're writing about – everything has to be planned in advance, and time is limited, so you have to make good use of every little bit of it that you are allotted in these special places, whether libraries or historical sites.

In other words, research is difficult and she takes it very seriously.

Dave Luckett is honest when considering the marketability of his work. 'I would have thought that [considering marketability is] an excellent method of producing a bad novel. If Spain in the seventeenth century interests you, write about that. Wishing you were somewhere else is certain to beget the same wish on the reader.' He is equally honest about considering his readers. 'The novels above were written without any idea of what readers might like.' And as for research, 'Who cares, so long as there is a substantial opinion that you can go with? Fifth to sixth-century Britain is basically a blank, apart from a little church history, but every list of every publisher contains a new Arthurian novel, and most of them are said to be a new take on "the historical Arthur". The Ricardian novel, which seeks to exculpate or eulogise Richard III, is almost a subgenre in itself, despite the fact that the idea rests on, shall we say, shaky evidence and requires the rejection of better evidence. But who cares?'

Given Luckett's long-term interest in history, this 'Who cares?' is somewhat misleading. Luckett writes in genres (speculative fiction) where historical accuracy is less essential and he writes from a position of fair historical understanding. He can therefore afford not to care, which is quite different to the writer of historical fiction with active fans and a genre that requires a closer adherence to known history. The detail of Luckett's answer, where he explains the main factors at play in his writing, demonstrates that his particular background and interests and his choice of genre put his initial response in perspective. He says, 'But apart from great fiction, the most important things, for me, were general reading of decent historians and science fiction fandom. A. J. P. Taylor and Macauley and Bishop Gardiner and Frank Stenton fed my desire to know what was going on beneath the dates and names and battles and Acts of Parliament. Fandom, with its wide catholic tolerance for anything reasonably harmless, was the origin of my certainty that you can write about anything you want to any way you want to. (That doesn't mean that people have to read you, of course.)' While Luckett refers specifically to speculative fiction fandom, 'fandom' can also point to the very different audience interaction between speculative fiction writers and their readers and those of historical fiction. The nature of the audience engagement and the nature of the genre are significant factors in what history the writer chooses and in how they use it.

Chaz Brenchley takes quite a different view when he explains that:

> I guess I will have thought 'I could sell this', when I first thought of a Crusader fantasy. Certainly my US agent said one of the reasons she could sell it in the States was because they could put knights with swords on the cover. After that, I followed my usual trick of going my own way and becoming progressively less commercial. They tried to sell the Ottoman books as harem romances, and largely failed; the Chinese series, my US agent asked me very seriously not to write at all, on the grounds that every few years a bold or naive editor tries an Oriental fantasy, and every time it fails ...

The personality of the writer is the key factor. The careful awareness of audience and of research belongs to the same authors that had deeply emotive engagements with history. Except where they didn't. Brian Wainwright, for instance, explains that he had 'No conscious influence; I write principally for myself.' He also points out that 'The opinions of other authors generally lead me to do the opposite – I do what I have to do!' The human factor emerges over and over again in the author interviews.

If a market view were key to the decisions of writers, it would show up in other answers. Sally Odgers says, however, about popular settings, 'I call these "box office settings" and unfortunately, I almost never use one. I'm interested in places and times that haven't been done to death.' She does respond to the market and to publishing needs, but she makes a clear distinction between her relationship with history and the relationship someone else wants her to have with history when she says 'if I'm writing on spec, I please myself. That's dangerous, but this part of my writing is my "real" stuff ... I actually make a living from commissioned stuff.'

Odgers is not a specialist historical fiction writer (she writes historical fiction, but these books fit into a larger practice that covers a wide range of novel genres, including speculative fiction) and, again, this shows in her interaction with readers. 'Readers rarely bother to let me know about their preferences in times/places.'

Both Robyn Starkey and Catherine Butler share the sense that market potential is less important than personal interest in selecting a subject. Starkey explains, 'I am not writing for a mass market – I am only really writing for myself and one or two readers. I found a publisher who wants to publish literary and eclectic work with some relationship to fantasy, so that seems like a good partnership.' She elucidates that 'I write what interests me; what I want to read.' Butler is down to earth in saying, essentially, the same: 'I'm hopelessly uncommercial.' Research is a more important factor, but influenced by quite specific personal conditions. 'I work as a university lecturer,' she points out, 'and therefore have pretty good access to such materials and the skills and contacts needed to find them.' This reinforces the importance of the individual, their interests and their circumstances as unexpressed factors that lie behind the formal.

This can be seen most clearly in the total impossibility Ross Hamilton found in addressing any factors that influence his writing. 'I don't think I can really answer the following [list of factors]. I write about what I like and find interesting, am influenced by what I have read, and can only research things that I can access research materials.'

Felicity Pulman sums up the general approach of historical fiction writers when she says:

> I write novels to tell the stories that I need to tell, the stories that fascinate me, that have captured my imagination and that won't free me until they've been written to my satisfaction. Anything else is secondary, including marketability, accessibility and quality of research materials, and reader and publisher preference (although it's always nice to be appreciated!).

Chris Andrews summarizes the more pragmatic speculative fiction writers when he says:

> Marketability is very important to me. I want to sell what I write, and to reach the largest possible audience. I'm happy to cater to what readers want. A lot of mass-market fantasy is written with a Middle Ages-type background, so I'm catering to those readers. My target audience seems to like to be entertained, first and foremost. Lots of action and adventure, uncertainty and a sense of tension. I write for the mass market – which is what publishing houses in general tend to cater for. I'll cater to an individual publishing house or editor when the time comes – and I'll be happy to change things if I believe it will help sell the story. I find the views of my peers very useful in several ways. They can often pick up on things I may have missed – typos, plot mistakes, things I've forgotten or gotten wrong. However, I tend to accept different viewpoints with an eye to an individual's reading and writing preferences, and accept or reject suggestions based on what I know about them. What I don't know or have difficulty finding out, I make up.

At the time of writing up these questionnaires in 2015, Andrews had only recently sold his first novel to a small publishing house whereas the writers who wrote from the less pragmatic view (such as Chadwick and Pulman) have had more than one novel published by major houses. Brenchley is the only writer interviewed whose career and approach challenges this pattern, for he writes successfully with the market in view, combining his passion for the subject with a pragmatic approach to what is likely to sell. He achieves this balance by suggesting several works to his agent and writing the one his agent prefers (personal communication, 2011). This suggests that the industry may be less intuitive than it seems, that publishers may want novels that suit a market and might explain that this is what they are after, but that the other factors are more important. Unfortunately, exploring publishing in any depth is beyond the scope of this work, but the publication history of these writers strongly suggests that the relationship between writer perception and the industry demands is very complex.

Sophie Masson is another commercially successful novelist. She writes mainly historical fantasy and thus fits at the pragmatic end of the spectrum in a perfect world where all writers fit into simple classifications. In reality, however, her publishing history is solid and the factors that she considers belong more at the historical fiction end than at the speculative fiction end. This demonstrates that the key factor in commercial success for a novel containing a significant historical component is probably that emotive connection with the history in the novel. 'It just depends what story I'm interested in,' she says, and 'I mostly please myself and the demands of the story I'm creating, but obviously I'm aware of what people have liked in the past. Obviously if [the publisher is] not interested, they're not going to take it; but I don't really think about that much, I just try to pitch the story itself to them – you can get people enthusiastic about anything if you're passionate enough.'

This is the key to it. It is the passion of the writer that generates the commercial interest when looking at the subject from the writer's perspective.

This explains Debra Kemp's answer, for she published against interesting odds:

> Nothing on your list really had an impact on my writing. I'm writing what I must write, in spite of all the factors against me: Arthurian fiction doesn't do well in the market, etc. I just had to keep writing and submitting because I believe in my character and her uniqueness within the Arthurian literature. It took seven years and 207 rejections to finally find a publisher willing to take a chance.

In bringing some of the tools novelists use in their writing into dialogue with how writers perceive their work, it becomes obvious that the tools are seldom used with careful intent. Passion is more likely to inform the use of history in fiction than an attempt to sell a book to a particular market using careful selection of technique to reinforce the market's needs. The ramifications of this will be explored further in the next chapter, where we examine the way a writer develops the world of the novel.

CHAPTER 3

Constructing the world of the novel:
The research trail

Now we move to the rather more difficult reality of how a writer constructs a world for a novel using history. First will be an overview of where fiction writers gain their chief body of understanding and how this is interpreted from a novelist's point of view.

Hsu-Ming Teo (2011: 306) points out that, although the worlds of novels are closed, 'For most practising historians however, historical writing is not a hermetically sealed world; it exists in an ongoing conversation with past, current and future historical writing.' While it is possible to argue that this situation also applies to fiction (with novels existing in ongoing conversations) the truth is that the conversations novels have with each other are quite different to the conversations histories engage in with other histories. A key difference is in the focus of the narrative: in a novel, the history is not a central focus and indeed for many writers it is not a part of the discussion at all. Essentially, their aim is to share narratives and explore narratives, with the development of a complex and dynamic relationship with history being a minor factor.

This does not mean that novels do not participate in historical discourse. The vast majority of them participate differently, however, to historiographical work. The focus in the novel is on the story, with characters and plot. Presenting what is known of a period is not as essential for the purpose of the novelist as it is for that of the historian, and very seldom does a novel enter into historical discourse directly by adding to knowledge about a precise subject. Although generally separated from formal historical discourse, however, the world created for the novel is heavily dependent on a conversation with history (for a study of this see Polack, 2014). Some even share a discourse concerning history that moves outside the boundaries of specific works. Their main approach, however, is narrative, not discursive or theoretical.

For example, the work of Elizabeth Chadwick generally explores the political and social history of twelfth-century England. This history is not her prime focus, however. Her works are narratives concerning the stories of people such as Eleanor of Aquitaine and her family. The political and social history is part of the stories she tells about these people. The history is subordinate to the story.

Likewise Kate Grenville in *The Secret River* (2005) offers an interpretation of Australian colonial life in Sydney. Grenville explores some of the relationships of her novel with the work of historians in her non-fiction work *Searching for the Secret River* (2005). In the novel itself, however, these issues are part of the background to the story. While Grenville's reinterpretation of her family's colonial origins underpins the narrative in *The Secret River*, the focus in the novel is upon the main characters and their lives, with the historical discussion and the research notes confined to the non-fiction work. This separation of function between the novel and the book about the investigation behind the novel demonstrates that even when a writer participates in the historical discourse, the formal discussion on matters relating to the novel generally happens outside the fictional work.

Participating in historical discourse does not necessarily mean researching as a historian would. The group of writers were asked what sort of sources they used. Most of the fiction writers depended far more heavily on secondary sources than primary. For some of them primary sources were almost non-existent: Debra Kemp, for example, writes about a fifth-century Arthur, and a fifth-century Arthur cannot be demonstrated using the historical record for there is no fifth-century Arthur in any part of the historical record. For many others, primary sources were only available in limited quantities and in translation.

The results of this section of the interviews cannot be extrapolated to all writers who use history in their world building. It is, in fact, quite specific to writers who focus on historical periods and places using languages that are no longer current. For Elizabeth Chadwick's Medieval English settings she would need Old English, Middle English, Latin and Old French to access the complete range of primary sources available, and would also need specialist palaeographical and diplomatics skills to access and interpret those that have not been edited by modern scholars. When asked about her research, Chadwick admits to using mainly published primary sources, with the vast majority of them in translation rather than in the original language. She is thus more dependent on secondary sources for the world building aspect of her research than a writer such as Kate Grenville who uses more recent history, for Chadwick's secondary sources contain the scholarship concerning the inaccessible primary sources that she most needs.

All of the writers studied use secondary sources, often extensively. Very few use more than a select few of the most accessible primary sources. Chadwick is exceptional in the number of primary sources she accesses: most use fewer. Chadwick does, however, represent her genre. In their answers to a question about their sources, historical fiction writers are more likely to report using a wider number of primary sources (in translation or not) than speculative fiction writers. All are more dependent on popular studies and secondary sources than on primary sources to establish the world of their novel.

The balance between primary and secondary sources is significantly different to that of historians. There is, however, a more fundamental difference in how writers of fiction research. Research for fiction is based on many of the same technical assumptions as research for history, but the focus on story means that other stories are also valid sources. Writers will use fiction as a research tool to establish their understanding of the setting for their novel.

They were asked about this in the context of factors that have been strongly influential on their own work. All authors read academic works and popular non-fiction as part of the research for their subject. What is of interest at this point is what kinds of fiction they use and what approach they take.

Elizabeth Chadwick was profoundly influenced by historical fiction. She says that 'I remember reading Roberta Gellis' Roselynde Chronicles, Cecelia Holland's *Hammer For Princes* and Sharon Penman's *Here Be Dragons* and thinking "Yes, this is the sort of accessible and accurate historical fiction that I'd like to write" – and in fact was writing at the time. I just needed to do some growing up and learn to write!'

Nicole Murphy is another writer who is deeply influenced by fiction:

> I love reading historical fiction because I feel like I'm learning while I'm enjoying a
> great story. There are a few things I hate: one, when I see an obvious mistake because
> the author hasn't done the research and two, when the author is obviously so proud
> of the research they have done that they feel compelled to share every single bit of
> their research. If I wanted to read a history book, I would get one.

For Dave Luckett, too, reading fiction was a given for fiction writers. 'Conan
Doyle and C.S. Forester and George MacDonald Fraser and Mary Renault
and Alexandre Dumas taught me to write historical fiction, which sounds
fearfully conceited, but notice, I'm not saying how successful they were.'
Sandra Worth explains that she:

> ... fell in love with Anya Seton's *Katherine* as a child, and that book threw open the
> door to English medieval history for me. As far as a list of all fiction I have read, that
> would be impossible, as I was reading Henry James, Edgar Allan Poe, Victor Hugo,
> Dickens, Dumas et al. from the age of ten onwards, and still re-read them. (Currently
> I've just finished re-reading *Les Misérables*, and am now re-reading Homer's Odyssey
> for the third time). I continue to favor the classics, and though I read many of the pre-
> eighties bestsellers, I don't care much for the moderns (since the eighties) except for
> Crichton, because the market changed and the quality of the writing was not the same.

Felicity Pulman said in a straightforward fashion that 'I enjoy reading his-
torical fiction and also crime novels, so I've been influenced by e.g. Ellis
Peters' Brother Cadfael series, A.E. Marston's Doomsday series and Sharon
Penman's *When Christ and His Saints Slept*.'

Given the low status of modern fiction as a historical source for earlier periods, the question of how writers researched using fiction was also
approached indirectly, by asking how important fiction was to them and
about the influence of other fiction on their work. The answers to this question demonstrate that, while most writers use fiction to help understand a
period, the way they use it is complex. Novels are not simply a replacement
for primary and secondary sources.

Michael Barry said that reading fiction was 'very important – I greatly
enjoy rewritings of history, in which the author inserts new events between
the cracks of known history. Craig Cormick is one local [Australian]

example; George R. R. Martin's *Fevre Dream* is another; however, I detest Harry Turtledove for no discernible reason.' The framework for his own fiction also comes from 'fiction written in and around the researched period plus diaries/letters/logs etc. for what people would be reading/thinking'. The distinction between modern fiction and fiction contemporary with his setting suggests that many of his dismissals of historical research may not be reliable as a guide to how seriously he takes his research.

Helen Hollick is influenced by fiction, but in a slightly different fashion:

> I was unimpressed by the majority of fiction concerning 'King Arthur' as nothing fitted *my* idea of him – hence I decided to write my own. Ditto King Harold, was fed up with English history starting with William the Conqueror – also fed up with general view of history that William was a 'good thing' for England. He wasn't. He was a murdering, usurping tyrant who had no right, whatsoever to the English throne. Influenced heavily by Rosemary Sutcliff.

Robyn Starkey, likewise, admitted influence from reading novels, but warned that although they are 'Definitely an influence,' they were 'Sometimes positive, sometimes negative (i.e. "I don't want to write that kind of trash").' Sally Odgers was also cautious when she explains, 'Sometimes I get interested in a place/period because of what I've read, but that's often non-fiction'.

Not all writers count fiction as critical to their writing. Brian Wainwright is far more dubious about chasing the influence of modern fiction on his own work, as is Sophie Masson. Masson's answer to the question was that she was 'not really' influenced, while Wainwright delved further into the question. 'At a sub-conscious level I think it must have an influence; I think my writing contains traces of several authors I particularly admire, but I am not sure this could ever be analysed.'

Catherine Butler is also cautious when she says, 'I'm sure this seeded my mind in various ways. A book by Alan Garner entitled *Red Shift* bears some resemblances to [a particular work of] mine (most obviously the tri-partite chronology), but fairly superficial ones.'

There appears to be no genre or stylistic link to the way authors were influenced by other fiction writers. Some were openly joyous about the influence of fiction on their historical work, some considered it a place to start from rather than something to emulate, and others were simply not certain. They all, however, accepted that they were, as fiction writers, influenced by other fiction. This influence does not appear to be linked to the level of formal education of the writers. What is important is that modern fiction concerning the place and time of interest plays an active part in informing the views on that place and time of most of the writers interviewed.

However influential it is, taking story ideas and characters from fiction is not sound historical method. While it would be useful to be able to assess how these writers use primary sources in their research, only two of them admitted to using primary sources. This, as we have seen, has several potential causes, not all of which are related to the author's interest in formal historical research. Few of these writers have reading knowledge of languages other than English; for others, there is also the issue of access to material. Kathleen Cunningham Guler admits this when she explains, 'Living in a small, rural town that doesn't have a large library, I've collected hundreds of academic and popular non-fiction books to aid in my research. Textbooks are usually too general and not as useful.' In assembling her own library, she is reliant on books that are available to buy. The hundreds of books she has access to direct her research in a far more specific way than the thousands of books that would be available on her period and place in a major library.

Guler was not atypical. The vast majority of the writers were heavily reliant on secondary sources available locally. Only a small number (Chadwick and Wainwright, for example) undertake research of a similar level to that of a historian.

While all authors use specialist work to a degree, the burden of research appears to be much heavier for historical fiction writers than for writers of speculative fiction, in that historical fiction writers are more likely to undertake a long-lasting and wide-ranging research programme as part of their work for the novel. Some speculative fiction writers undertook significant research but Chris Andrews and Michael Barry had the same opinion about the whole research process. As Barry says, 'I go and find what I need. If finding materials is too difficult, I make them up myself!'

**

A key reason for the balance between primary and secondary sources, and for reading modern fiction as part of the preparation that a writer will do for a novel, relates to the nature of the novel itself. Novels do not present arguments or descriptive overviews of a period or place: they tell story.

All stories rest on the believability of the world in which they are set. Whether one relates the building and use of the world back to theory (for example, through considering such concepts as poeisis and mimesis, as discussed in Jaeger, 2011) or simply describes the world as Tolkien's Middle Earth or McCaffrey's Pern, the universe of the novel must be credible for the novel to meet the needs of its reader.

Some of the credibility of the world relies on formal research, and we have seen that all writers questioned undertake formal research for their work. This formal research is, however, mainly preliminary and not the only factor in building a credible world. (If it were the central factor, the lack of access to primary sources and to big research libraries would be a far greater problem for writers.) Story is what gives this status to the world: if the work can be made to look seamless in terms of story, the lack of access to a particular source to demonstrate that a particular element is verifiable becomes irrelevant. Thus many writers use techniques that disguise the gaps in their built world. Glenda Larke's archipelago in her Isles of Glory series of fantasy novels depends heavily on the ability of the reader to follow the cycle of cloth manufacture from animal to clothing: the various types of fibre are used to unify several distinct societies and to reduce Larke's reliance on complex world building. The author needs to create a world that is convincing, not necessarily complete. The nature of credibility and how it is achieved will be discussed in more depth later, however, it must be noted here that it is a critical factor in what research the writer undertakes and how it is woven into the story.

Beneath the story, however, lies the need to give the reader the perception of a functioning world. If a writer is to build a functioning world from historical sources or from histories, they will rely heavily on someone else's interpretations of a shared understanding of the past. It is quite different from the creation of a world out of raw material.

The form and function of the historical narrative being written by the historian plays an active role in how sources are interpreted. Statistical averages, shifts in currency, trade figures, census data, shifts in wage levels, purchasing power of individual households and similar data sets are important tools for a historian. The data sets of historians are discussed in Howell and Prevenier (2001: 50ff) and underpin many studies by giving indicative values upon which specific interpretations can be based or providing contexts for broader social and economic analysis. These same data sets can be dangerous tools for a novelist who lacks sufficient technical understanding to break them down. This is the point at which the skills difference manifest between a writer who knows a great deal about the Middle Ages and a writer who is a professional historian.

This helps to explain why writers use secondary sources and even other fiction to help establish their period and place: by relying on the interpretations of others, fiction writers do not have to accumulate the same range of technical skills as a historian researching the same place and time. How the data is used to inform the story counts (for instance, Glenda Larke's trade routes for her various fabrics give the reader a very good sense of how her islands and their trade products relate to each other both politically and socially) more than the author's capacity to read and interpret historical data sets and documents.

Method and approach are key. My own work with writers suggests that, to create good historical fiction, a writer must do three things:

1) Disengage themselves sufficiently from the present to understand that history includes a very large element of cultural shift
2) Build an intellectual understanding of a period and place, usually through research, and
3) Develop an affective understanding of the subject, possibly like the one many fiction writers develop for their central characters (internalization)

In addition to this, if a writer is to participate actively in historical discourse, there is a fourth requirement:

4) Maintain intellectual rigour while creating an effective interpretation of the other categories.

The last category is not relevant to most fiction writers (as discussed in Polack, 2014), because they seldom engage in full scholarly discourse on the history in their fiction.

Is it possible to quantify the amount of research done or the time spent?

Chaz Brenchley articulates most clearly how complex research can be for a writer and how difficult to describe simply. The research he describes does not follow standard historical method. It is only in small part about asking a question, defining parameters, finding appropriate research materials and answering the question. Brenchley sees research as complex. He explains that:

> ... you need to understand my process. And its evolution. Before I began the Outremer novels, I spent the best part of a year reading everything I could find about the Crusades, and making copious notes. After I finished, I realised that I had never once referred to any of those notes, despite my appalling memory. It's not about accuracy, I never need to get things right on that level. For *Selling Water*, I read everything I could find on the Ottoman Empire, and took no notes at all. It's about filtration; the stories pass through my conceived notion of their setting, which is both well-informed but ill-retentive. The works I make this way are referential rather than descriptive; the fantasy is more important than the historical element (though the character/relationship interchange trumps both).

> The Daniel Fox books are an elaboration of this process. I first went to Taiwan ten years ago, and I've been doing the background research ever since: which includes the usual reading-everything, but also learning Chinese ('how can I hope to understand the way they think, if I don't understand the tool they use to think with?'), spending more time there and with Taiwanese elsewhere.

Historical research method is a part of the way writers use history in their fiction, but it is secondary to how story develops, because story is more important. Brenchley's process demonstrates that he was seeking to understand the place and time from a direction suitable for his writing: this is why his articulation of the relative importance of the fantasy compared with the historical elements for *Selling Water* is a critical aspect of his own description of his research.

Most writers interviewed found it difficult to describe the amount of research done or even to quantify the time spent. Sandra Worth suggested that it was a third of her total time spent working on a project and Elizabeth Chadwick said that for a familiar setting:

> ... about a month to six weeks before I start writing and continuously throughout all the drafts of the novel. I probably research for between half an hour and an hour every day of the year i.e. I always read a research book at bedtime and I research specific subjects in my study during the course of writing.

Both of these authors write historical fiction and these answers were typical of historical fiction writers, both those interviewed for this project and the published interviews consulted. Even when they found it hard to quantify the research, they spent a considerable amount of time engaged in it. They considered this groundwork important both to plotting their novels and also to developing their characters.

Fantasy writers, on the other hand, do not spend the same amount of time undertaking basic research. At one end of the scale is Dave Luckett who has, it must be pointed out, a degree in history, but who explains that the time he spends in researching for a novel is 'None. Oh, I might look up a detail here or there, but only *inter alia*.' Speculative fiction writer Maxine McArthur says the time spent on basic research is 'a small proportion of the pre-writing time, about the same proportion of the research conducted while writing (because things crop up as you write that you didn't realise at first you'd have to research)'. She also has university qualifications in history.

The numbers interviewed are insufficient to know if these patterns apply to historical fiction as opposed to speculative fiction in general, but it is interesting to note that there is a clear differentiation between the two groups of writers.

Fiction writers write to contemporary narrative norms. The research that they do to build the world of their novel and to make it believable for readers is channelled to meet those norms. This is a key reason why one group of writers might undertake more initial research than another.

The body of understanding used by writers to build the world of their novel is much easier to interpret when it rests on modern assumptions concerning a particular place or time. A common problem of novels that use history is that of presenting modern characters in ancient dress or modern stereotypes of a period that wore ancient dress. An interesting example of both of these is Fiona Avery's *The Crown Rose* (2005), which uses modern manners and social expectations to tell a story set in thirteenth-century France. While the main character, Isabelle, is a member of the thirteenth-century French royal family, her characterization is distinctly modern, as are many of her actions. The modernization goes as far as using modern French as the language for some of the dialogue. Avery nevertheless has a six-page afterword explaining her research and where her story intersects with known fact: the history is sufficiently important to warrant an explanation, even when the author's interpretation from their sources is at a far remove from the historian's understanding of that time and place.

What Avery has done with her world building (why her historical interpretation differs so significantly from most historians') is to rely upon her assumptions concerning the Middle Ages when the sources she used did not address her narrative needs. This is important to note, for the reliance upon assumptions has impact on the building of the world of the novel (which will be discussed later), but it also has immediate consequences for the detail she uses to bring her novel to life. She obviously did not consult thirteenth-century manuals of etiquette when her characters shake hands rather than kissing, but she still feels the need to explain her research.

Some of these differences between writers are linked to their personality, that is, they relate to how much work a specific writer is willing to undertake. As we have seen, the work choices of writers vary. Some of the differences between writers relates to the nature of the work undertaken, for example, how analytical it is and how much historical data is taken on trust and how much is questioned by the writer themselves. Some, on the other hand, depends on the work of historians of the period the writer is researching, those secondary sources upon which so many of these writers heavily depend. A writer can work cleverly and hard, and still have crucial gaps in the historical backdrop.

Where precisely does the writer's information concerning the past come from? What are their sources? While this has briefly been discussed, it is important to look into this subject in more detail.

It would be easy (but not useful) here to list types of sources, ranging from government documents to personal letters. These lists can be created very easily. They can vary significantly from a few items to being many pages long. They do not, however, address where a writer mainly gets their information for most novels. Different writers use different sources, even when writing on the same subject.

As we have seen, some fiction writers conduct considerable research using a wide range of sources and investigating primary sources (Mary Sharratt does this, for instance, for her 2010 novel *Daughters of the Witching Hill*) and some do not (Avery, again, provides a useful example).

There is no single path to research for a novel and there is no single set of sources. There is no novelistic equivalent of a formal literature review as used as a part of scholarly history using standard methodologies to ensure that novelists begin at the same point to progress discussion along known lines.

The research a fiction writer undertakes relies less on the paths earlier travelled (although they are not independent of these paths) than on the nature of the novel, the nature of the author's relationship with history and the needs of a specific novel. The assumptions of writers and the way(s) they interact with the work of historians thus deeply inform the history in a given novel. However, it was established through the interviews, through informal discussions, and through examination of author notes in volumes and on websites, that many writers begin with popular histories and with textbooks or websites that describe the chosen place and time. These resources give them a framework for further research if they feel it is necessary.

Historians continually discuss the nature of historical fact, how we come to know about it and where we get our interpretations from. Only some writers of fiction are interested in these questions.

Historians do not do their work in order to provide complete worlds for writers of fiction. By and large, the method of writing history in a manner that is suitable for academics separates the past from precisely that cultural element that the writer needs, and therefore the writer has to track across many sources to discover these links and to use them effectively. The difference between the research time spent by an Avery and a Chadwick is quite obvious in the narrative itself, but the gaps in research by modern historians also shows. Debra Kemp's work, set in fifth-century Britain, covers a period about which we know little of social customs and everyday behaviour. All the interaction between characters is thus entirely invented: there were no secondary sources that were suitable and very little historical research at all on these subjects. Fiction writers are, for the most part, dependent on their cultural and intellectual environments.

The other area that may demonstrate research gaps is, oddly, voice. The 'voice' of a writer is the quality in the writing that creates the subjective perception that this writer speaks uniquely. It can be built up through use of adjectives and adverbs, through sentence types, through use of different senses in the writing, through use of dialect and so on. It is complex to establish, but a clear or unique voice is often an important part of a writer's toolbox for publishing and marketing their work.

Writers often use a particular voice to shape a belief or an interpretation in the mind of the reader. Hilary Mantel uses the present tense as the foundation for the voice of *Wolf Hall*, suggesting that the novel is set in a historic present and thus intimates that Thomas Cromwell is a modern protagonist. Voice within a novel is one of the complex means of creating a character and fixing them within the world and within the plot. A strong character voice instantly differentiates a character from another and enables story to be woven more effectively.

Voice can serve a variety of plot functions. If a writer, for instance, has chosen an inappropriate voice (and here we return to Avery's novel and the modern voice of Isabelle) it masks the level of research the writer has undertaken. The novel then relies on the skill of the plotting and on levels of tension to indicate its historicity. This is typically what happens in a thriller (Michael Crichton's 1999 novel *Timeline*, for instance) when the plot is pre-eminent and the history falls into place as a part of the tension-building. It is a clear narrative choice for some writers (such as Crichton) but also the default to which other writers fall (such as Avery) when other narrative elements are insufficient to communicate the level of historical research.

It is important to note that voice is never a neutral player. It can point to research or it can mask it or it can point to flaws in research or to flaws in the conceptualization of the history in the novel. It speaks for the author's work. The writer communicates through it and therefore it colours how the reader discovers character, plot, and whether the research undertaken is viable and visible.

That research, however, still derives from outside sources. Voice is a vehicle for interpretation, not the place where the data and its interpretation comes from. It is, however, key to that interpretation, it enables the writer to present someone who is insightful giving an explanation, or a traveller seeing things for the first time, or someone ignorant being led through crucial background or plot elements.

To summarize, the writer draws an understanding of history from their research as part of the formulation of a story. The way that this is communicated to the reader colours the history within the novel, thus presenting a picture of a historical place and time that is unique to that writer. At the heart of this uniqueness are the writers' methods, and, just as importantly, the writers' sources.

***

Some types of writing by historians lend themselves more straightforwardly to the needs of novelists and are thus less likely to add to this chasm between the needs of the two groups. Cultural history, focussing on the specifics of culture (all aspects of culture, not merely high culture, that is to say, folk culture as well as music and mathematics) in a temporal dynamic, works somewhat better than many other forms of history as a place to find a setting. This is because the interests of the cultural historian (daily life, personal needs and interests, family, time, space) are all essential aspects of a good novel.

While cultural histories are quite different narratives to novels, the commonalities are sufficient to make them more accessible to fiction writers building a world and telling a story. It is likely that this creates overlapping narratives, where the stuff of daily life, for instance, is likely to be important to both. This is likely to be due to a complex mix of shared assumptions (*this material belongs to folk life* and *that material is the stuff of daily living*) and the colour that cultural history can bring to fictional narrative. As an example of this latter, it is much easier to illustrate the nature of a character's medical skills using actual remedies than using general statements. Thus, when Felicity Pulman needed to demonstrate the Anglo-Saxon background of her protagonist, Janna, in her series (The Janna Mysteries), she referred to Stephen Pollington's book on leechcraft (Pollington, 2001) (private communication, 2009).

Some of the theoretical issues addressed by historians in their various kinds of writing are also important for writers of fiction, whether the historical writing is political history, ethnohistory, theory of history or something else. A crucial aspect of world building is the one that is invisible unless specifically addressed: addressing assumptions.

One of the primary tools of scholarly historians and one of the reasons for the importance of scholarly apparatus is to enable other scholars to examine the road travelled and for all parties to examine the assumptions brought into the interpretation of research. This is discussed at its most basic level in introductions to historical method and theory for undergraduates, such as E.H. Carr (1987) or John Tosh (2006). It enables discourse, but it also enables the dynamic of scholarly history, because examining assumptions is just as important as new evidence for enabling change in scholarship.

Throughout the interviews, however, only a few writers demonstrated the capacity to articulate their relationship to sources in this manner, and the ones who did were all either writers of historical fiction or writers with academic qualifications in history, save for Brenchley. The usefulness of a wide range historical research to writers is not intuitive, therefore, but learned. The examination of assumptions depends upon skills that are not essential to fiction writers who use history, therefore, for if they were essential, more writers would manifest them. This means that the writer's use of sources is quite different to the historian's in a number of ways, not only in relative use of primary and secondary sources.

CHAPTER 4

Constructing the world of the novel: The nature of the narrative and of the world-build

Although 'world building' is a concept used mainly by writers of speculative fiction, it is a useful concept for describing the nature of research undertaken for a novel. The description of this process as 'world building' is often intended quite literally (inasmuch as a science fictional or fantasy world needs to be 'built' to the level of reality required by readers), but on a more metaphorical level it can be applied to the task facing any writer seeking to create any world, including one that uses history.

There is no single method for approaching world building and the array of techniques suggested by writers and educators range from intuitively developing specific detail, to running computer programs to build the fabric of the world. Some authors give checklists of items that a world might need (clothes, food, animals, languages) and others suggest shortcuts. A common checklist for writers of speculative fiction is a lengthy list of questions provided by the Science Fiction Writers of America and devised by fantasy writer Patricia C. Wrede. The questions range from climate and crops, through customs and cultures, to calendars. Some writers literally build the physical world (Russell Kirkpatrick, for instance, who is a practising cartographer as well as a writer of epic fantasy, has full detail of landforms and wind patterns and related matters for his fantasy worlds) while others loosely base the world they write in on one they are familiar with (George R. R. Martin's physical world for Westeros is very similar to England, for instance.)

World building is the stage of writing when a novelist can most easily address their own assumptions, whether these concern the washing habits of Londoners in sixteenth-century England as in Dan Abnett's *Triumff* (2009) or the way a character buttons their garment (and that the garment has buttons) in an alternate reality or off-world fantasy such as in Chris Wooding's Braided Path series. It is the moment in which the writer decides just how much new cloth there will be in the fabric of their world-for-the-novel. Where they do not consciously make the decision to use new cloth, then old will dominate. Old cloth includes tropes and figures used in similar types of novels as well as the regular assumptions derived from popular history. The importance of these assumptions to modern popular interpretations and use of a period can be seen in relation to the Middle Ages in Polack and Kania (2015) and Harris and Grigsby (1999–2001).

It is almost impossible to address all one's preconceived assumptions prior to writing a novel. The methods by which some writers avoid the most glaring errors, however, are very useful in helping us understand how a writer builds the world of their novel and how they move into the writing itself. It gives us a deeper understanding not only of processes, but of the underlying culture of narrative. Instead of assuming that, for example, in the eighteenth century everyone read Voltaire, the writer could ask 'Where does Character A get their information about literature from? What (if anything) did they read or have access to?' These are the types of choices the writer makes, at the coalface. The assumptions that feed the choices for character, the focus of the character's view and the narrator's voice and, below that, how the world of the novel is communicated, provide the dynamic that translates the writer's sense of history into the story they are writing.

So, what are the deeper sources of these assumptions? They can be expressed through dividing the historical sense into broad categories. These categories underpin such apparently simple decisions such as whether the character Jane acts in a certain way and whether her life is pure invention. They relate very closely to whether we have experienced an event, whether it is part of our lives, or whether it is a formal part of the historical record and if we know it mainly through that record or through narratives that draw on that record.

The first category is *experienced history*, that is to say, the history of any given individual. It is what we live through as human beings: what we remember, what we think about through our own experience. It derives from the experiences of an individual in his or her lifetime. By no means does it consist of every event in a person's life, or every event in the contemporary world. It is defined primarily through the remembering of it. If a child did not read of the death of J. F. K. and it made no other impact on him or her at that time, then he cannot be said to have that particular death as a part of his experienced history. However, someone older might have heard of it and remembered it. In this case, that death would have been etched upon the memory of the person and would help form the development of his remembrance of the past. All of us possess it. Experienced history is at the root of the development of personal historical consciousness. We start to be interested in history, because we have started to live history.

It is a strong part of Western culture. In pre-modern England children helped walk boundaries so that, when they became adults, they could attest in court to the limit of those boundaries. It is referred to in fiction to indicate a closeness with the past. 'I was there. I was in this time and in this place.'

The second is *remembered history*. Remembered history is shared by more than one person. It incorporates aspects of experienced history but is relevant to a larger number of people. It is history shared by a particular cohort: going through a recession together, or living through World War II. It is recollections, the immediate shared history of any individual or group. Families add to it when they tell each other stories. Even coming home from school and telling of a great score or a funny joke can add to it. Remembered history changes continually; we reinterpret it throughout our lives as we experience things or learn more to add to it.

Remembered history acts as a bias, sometimes perceived, sometimes merely acted upon, a basis of semi-historical knowledge which can rest beneath choices and determine their direction. Understanding one's own background and biases is part of the training of most historians.

It is also the remembrance of events from a distant past in a culturally homogenous group, and their re-interpretation over time. Whilst they survive in the community as a whole and retain their cultural currency, they are part of the remembered past. Popular heroes such as Arthur and Robin Hood, popular stories such as the legends of Troy fit into this. This is the most important element in fantasy novels in particular: the shared culture is used by many writers to create the world of the novel.

This category is often inaccurate or imprecise for historians. They can analyse the legends, as Stephen Knight does in *Robin Hood: A Mythic Biography* (2009) but they have strict rules of evidence for discussing the reality of the hero.

Remembered history consists primarily of legendary history and the mythicization of the past. In many works of history it has a similar external appearance to more validated historical recounting, and thus it can be mistaken for 'history' by readers. Its importance for fantasy narratives (the use of mythic characters, of hero-stories) makes this a place where crossover can happen with astonishing ease, where the assumptions of the writer concerning the historical or mythic figure can help shape the story.

When knowledge of an aspect of history is held only by a few, it may fall into a third category: *learned history*. This is the history of specialists. Not only professional historians and archivists, but of anyone who undertakes the serious study of history.

Historical fiction writers have their own versions of learned history that vary according to how far they themselves have become specialist in a field through the research they have undertaken for their novels. Where they do not understand or know an element of learned history, they will replace it with something from one of the other histories that is derived from their own prior knowledge. It also changes the way historians read these records.

Historians do not just read texts: they evaluate them continually. This means that there is a crucial relationship between experienced history itself with personality, with literary norms and with why the work was written. It is the province of specialists and implies a particular relationship between an individual or group and sources not available to the community as a whole.

The role of the person who uses learned history is usually interpretative. Take the J. F. K. example. A historian might write a history of how the shooting happened, or how mood swung on international policy in the US because of it. A writer of fiction might interpret the event in terms of where a major character was on that day and how it affected her life.

Historical discourses, however, usually operate in a dynamic environment. Historiography and the awareness of change in historical narratives is a key aspect of the discipline. This can trap many fiction writers when they see the discipline of history as static because their use of it is confined to their personal approach to research, and is not underpinned with historical theory or method. For world building to be easy to use in a novel, stability is a great asset.

Most of the history a writer uses is therefore inherited from one place or another. It needs reinterpretation to meet the writer's needs. To reinterpret, they have to confront world views that do not conform with their own. In my analysis of the work of writers I have established that there are differences between:

1) Reality
2) Formal interpretations of reality to explain history through the novel
3) Informal interpretations of reality to explain history through the novel
4) Formal interpretations of reality to change history within the novel
5) Informal interpretations of reality to change history within the novel.

These classifications and their differences lie beneath the attempts of writers to determine what cultural constructs a character is likely to have. A character might have personal narratives that inform their actions and have consequences. This includes inner dialogues: 'I can do this but I can't do that.' In *Wolf Hall*, Mantel's focal character, Thomas Cromwell, has internal narratives that are not only striking, but which also delineate Cromwell's cultural constructs very clearly. For example (Mantel, 2010: 253), Cromwell thinks when he sees Henry draw his bow, 'I see now he is royal.' Cromwell's observation places Henry's royalty clearly in a warrior culture, and specifically, since the book uses English history, in a culture where the longbow has had success as a weapon of war. While this requires clarification by Cromwell to communicate the concept to readers (the rest of the paragraph is chiefly devoted to this elucidation), by placing the thought and observation in Cromwell's mind as a direct observation of the king's activity, Mantel delivers an insight into Cromwell's cultural constructs.

The actions of characters might be informed by religious narratives. The most common of these at times of great tribulation is, 'What will happen to me after I die?' Again, a character's answer to this question can have far-reaching implications for the plot of a novel.

Social narratives are also important. Does a character have a strong desire to fall in love, and does that cause them to create difficult social situation for themselves or to undertake a quest for romantic adventure? This type of narrative is particularly important across genres, for the way characters see themselves operating socially is something that emerges in all novels.

Other narratives that emerge include health narratives ('I must ignore minor ailments and finish this task'), work narratives (which can range from the fairytale 'I'm too beautiful to work and so I need to find a husband', to the quasi-historical 'No-one of my status undertakes manual labour'), to conflict narratives ('I am a member of a threatened minority and threatened and need to hide/defend myself').

How each writer addresses each narrative depends very much on a given novel and the preferences of the writer and the perceived market needs (these will be discussed in more detail later). Writers will, however, demonstrate patterns in their choices over a number of novels. For instance, Elizabeth Chadwick consistently writes novels set at a certain period of English history and concerning a certain level of society. Thus these narratives are very important for understanding a writer's relationship with history.

Many writers address these issues instinctively but mistakes ensue when instinct fails (for instance, Connie Willis' dislike of the Middle Ages caused her to create some unlikely situations in her 1992 novel *The Doomsday Book*). Moreover, as Cowart says (1989: 20): 'The inferior historical novel is positively gravid with information; the inferior historical novelist fails to subordinate raw history to art.'

Writers each carry a body of baggage in the form of prior understandings of the subjects they write about. This general knowledge is reinforced by the popular fiction many of them read as a part of their preparation to write. These assumptions influence the shape of the narrative. Where a writer reads almost wholly within a genre, it is likely that they will develop the skills they require almost intuitively from their reading and will then write without a high level of awareness concerning the language they manipulate or the story structure they use: the narrowness of their interests thus creates the style of their novel.

One of the authors interviewed to whom this applies is Nicole Murphy. She admits that she writes quickly and that she does not research the nature of story (personal communication, 2011). Most of her published novels fit a straightforward pattern of romantic fantasy. Her Dream of Asarlai trilogy, for example, has a loose base in Irish folklore but its main focus is upon lonely individuals (usually with supernatural ability) finding their soulmates. The secondary plot is adventure fantasy, with the individuals in question saving the Gadda (human-like fairies) from threats.

All this adds up to a complex reality for writers: world building is not simple research nor is it straightforwardly exploring the history that is crucial for the novel. It has stages and levels and making use of those cleverly enables the novelist to effectively use the world they have built.

***

Implied in the previous discussion is that world building is not simply a matter of building the background for the novel; it is also a matter of preparing for the act of writing the novel by confronting a series of challenges, some intellectual and some personal. This section will look closely at the three stages a writer must go through to fully internalize their understanding of history in order to write effective fiction, that is, in order to integrate research into fiction and make the research function within genre constraints. The stages have been developed through working with a significant number of writers over the last twenty years, and then checked against the work of other writers, including those interviewed for this project.

1. The beginner's approach (Berlitz School)

This is the stage when the writer knows so little of history that they make basic errors in terminology. Their understanding is superficial and their cognitive awareness is low. A good example of this (besides Avery, already mentioned) is the television series *Sleepy Hollow*, which has 'Middle English' spoken in the seventeenth century. The beginner's approach implies a superficial knowledge of historical information, without any understanding of its contexts. This means that the interpretation of the information is likely to be wrong; for instance, in the Sleepy Hollow case, the language that would have been spoken by the Roanoke settlers was Early Modern English.

2. The past as too foreign to understand emotionally

This is the stage when the writer has a solid intellectual grasp of the standard interpretation of the past or has a vast array of information about the past at their fingertips that is able to be flourished in the novel. It is, however, as if the author needs an interpreter to explain that the past s/he is delineating so carefully contains real people. Cognitive understanding is not balanced with an equal affective understanding. There is a lack of emotional affinity for the place and time, generally, leading to a superficial (but often detailed) depiction. An example of this is Kim Stanley Robinson's late Middle Ages in *Galileo's Dream* where the narrative includes assumptions of a naïve approach to science by most characters in the novel rather than a pre-modern approach.

3. The history used in the novel is sufficiently well understood that the story-telling and characterization can take prime place

This is the stage when cognitive and affective understanding of the place and time are both at the service of story. In novels at this stage of advancement, the writer has developed an understanding of the place and time in which the novel is set, and ceases to see it as a collection of data points.

This enables the writer to create their own historical interpretation. In maintaining the foreign language analogy, the novelist is able to operate at the level of a full interpreter: a good example is Hilary Mantel's *Wolf Hall*.

The problem of popular assumptions concerning the past also needs to be examined: it poses a dilemma for the writer, since the reading audience may often share such assumptions and yet they may well rest on a very poor understanding of the past. Robert Penn Warren (1969: 72) explains: 'We are stuck with the fact that life involved passions and concerns and antipathies and anguish about the materials of life itself – whatever goes on in our hearts and outside of ourselves. This is what good literature involves. If you couldn't carry these things into literature, literature would be meaningless.' This is the chief reason for the essential nature of the movement from the Berlitz stage to the primacy of the storytelling: it creates a story that is more authentic for the novelist. In the process, it may create better history, but this is not a given, since the intent of novelists is to create story and only a small percentage of novelists are attempting primarily to write history.

The critical pathway for writers from the Berlitz stage to the next is, of course, through research. In the interviews, the writers were asked 'How do you master your source material and make it part of your narrative?' Their responses give a good idea of how they consciously tackle the questions I have just discussed.

Michael Barry's approach was to 'Develop a good idea of the characters' voices, then write my "research notes" as if the characters themselves are encountering the source material', while Elizabeth Chadwick writes

> a very detailed synopsis at the outset so I more or less know my beginning, middle and end. This is based on the month or six weeks research beforehand. When I create setting, I use a tremendous amount of sensual input – sights, sounds, smells, etc. Obviously these have to be researched too! Dialogue shouldn't sound too modern. Good basic English will suffice. I am afraid that the flow of the story and the dialogue is down to my subconscious – the thing I was born with and I can't explain how I do it. It's just there.

She does not (and many writers do not) trace a conscious path to deeper understanding. The translation between knowledge and enough understanding to write fiction for Chadwick operates, as it does for the majority of the writers, at the instinctive level. Barry, in this, is atypical. Sandra Worth, for example, works in a similar way to Chadwick: 'My research gives me the information I need,' she explains, 'and subconsciously sets the scenes I'm going to use.'

Some writers are distrustful of their relationship with source material and the relationship other writers have with their source material. Dave Luckett explains:

> Nobody 'masters' the source material. I'm sure I don't, and I have the utmost suspicion of those who think they have. Anybody who has ever read history must be aware of how much of it is unknown or uncertain, and in how many places we can simply accept another interpretation. And above all, we are writing fiction. It really doesn't matter if it isn't quite like what actually happened, even if we think we know what that was. What matters is that it holds together; that the events are possible; that their implications follow; that the characters act, think and feel, not as we would act, think, or feel, but as we can believe they would.

Luckett also raises an important point about the relationship of the Berlitz understanding with dialogue. He explains:

> About dialogue: There is what I might call the Geoffrey Farnol school of historical dialogue, otherwise known as *Forsoothly*. There is also the idea that the characters should speak as we do. I try to steer a middle path. Dialogue is one of the most powerful weapons for the historical writer. Characters speak as they think, and how they think is a vital piece of exposition.

Dialogue is, however, not the only tool at the writer's disposal. Sally Odgers explains, 'I use small domestic detail ... for example, when describing Nan Poole's cottage in *Replay*, I mentioned her bees, swine and flowers. I had all kinds of trouble trying to find out if goats were in England at that point.'

A focus on these tools assists the writer in narrating even when the source material is not mastered. In fact, they explain why distrustful writers such as Luckett still comfortably use history in their fiction.

Catherine Butler provides a useful summary of the processes:

> I don't have any direct source material as such, since I'm not writing about a specific event or person, just a milieu, which I have researched from secondary sources. I'm a great believer in reading a lot and then letting it compost and break down for a

bit somewhere at the back of my mind. Sometimes research can give you new and useful ideas, but it's more common to find something that excites you greatly at the time and that you distort your whole book in order to shoehorn in, only to decide months later that it just didn't belong after all. Putting a bit of time between you and the research is the best way to calm down and avoid that 'over-researched' look. Ideally you should feel as at home in, and (in a way) as unexcited about, the medieval world as your own.

Writing, for all the authors interviewed, has a significant intuitive element, and research needs to be processed through this in order to be transformed, using a range of techniques, into character and plot. Sophie Masson explains this thus:

> I try to get to the heart of it; not to overload the narrative or dialogue with 'quaintisms' but to give a feel for the language and concerns of the period through a certain rhythm of words, or images and symbols current at the time. The novel must have 'texture' and the source material provides the thread for that; but it must be woven into a coherent story shape, and that can mean sometimes changing things a little. You can't become a prisoner of your source material or your novel dies; equally you can't just ignore it, or it feels unreal.

We have already seen Brenchley's complex processes: he has a near-complete balance of the cognitive and the affective. He achieves this, however, by creating his own story place rather than one that closely reflects known history. 'I read everything and take no notes,' he explains, 'so that the material just settles down into a general background feeling, which informs the language and the setting and the whole ambience of the book. I'm not sure I master anything, I just absorb it, and then the characters work within and emerge from that milieu.'

All this is background for understanding that writers progress in stages towards creating a good novel that uses history in a manner that creates a believable narrative. Where the history is poorly understood, it affects the credibility of the novel.

The past is foreign. The explanations given for events may not be in line with current history or may be underpinned by entirely inappropriate behaviour by characters. The writer has not learned to assess that source and its implications. The writer depends solely on their previous understanding of a place and time (their remembered past) and uses this to make the narrative feel real. It might be more easily accessible, but the finished novel says more about the time and place the writer knows than the time and place the writer has been researching.

Robert Penn Warren (1969) points out that the historian does not know their imagined world: they have not internalized it. This is arguable. Modern historiographical theory says that the historian is writing narrative (the work of Alun Munslow and Frank Ankersmit provide excellent examples of this): this entails emotional bonding and internalization. What Robert Penn Warren is indicating, however, is that the fiction writer's internalization is different in kind to that of the historian. 'The fiction writer must claim to *know* the *inside* of his world for better or for worse ... Historians are concerned with the truth *about*, with knowledge *about*, the fiction writer with knowledge *of*.' While modern historiography will dispute the precision of this boundary (and the special edition of *SPIEL* in 2011 is dedicated to such a discussion), it is nonetheless an accurate one and explains why the built world is shaped the way it is for writing and why the resources of the historian do not match those of the fiction writer.

While fiction can challenge historical theory, it seldom does so and, in fact, few fiction writers concern themselves with it. Those that do, more often write literary novels (which, for the purposes of this study are considered to be novels that do not fall easily within the genres listed earlier: a genre novel can be 'literary' in terms of the level of writing and characterization, while still formally being able to be considered a speculative fiction or historical fiction work) than historical fiction or fantasy. Novelists may challenge an interpretation of a given historical figure's character, for instance, as the number of novels concerning Richard III or Arthur demonstrates. These fictions are less interested in historiography than in emotional links with the past and the stories that history carries and reflect the views expressed by writers in previous chapters.

The critical problem with reader assumptions about the history a novel is based on arises if these assumptions are not met. The reader will then feel that the reader contract has not been met. The 'reader contract' is another of those nebulous ideas that many writers work with in order to produce professional work. It can constitute specific elements. The example most often given in speculative fiction circles is that when a reader hears a shoe drop in a story, they will expect to hear the pair of that shoe also drop. This is a device used by many writers to create tense moments, for instance, by including mention of a weapon early in the story and then later on having that weapon fired. It can equally be quite general: if the novel is a romance novel, then the reader expects the protagonist to develop a love interest. Sharon Kay Penman refers to the need to meet the reader contract obliquely in an interview for the literary magazine *Bibliobuffet* (Polack, 2011) as she discusses who she writes about and the approach she takes.

The problem with the reader contract and fiction is that history is less verifiable in fiction, that is to say that there is little or no academic apparatus enabling the reader to check the work of the writer. This means that popular assumptions of the period and how reliable the writer is seen to be on the subject are very important aspects of the presentation of history in a novel. For more on this verifiability see Dorrit Cohn's *The Distinction of Fiction* (2000).

Some periods are particularly notable for the difference between popular assumptions and the historical understanding. The Middle Ages has not only one of the largest gaps between the popular and the academic in this respect, but it is also one of the most common settings for English-language novels. Feudalism, for instance, is often depicted as something quite different to its complex and challenged reality. Some authors assume that all Europe was Christian, others assume that washing was a more modern invention. These and other misconceptions are dealt with by historians on a continuing basis, but they still operate in novels when writers fail to address them.

Writers are builders and interpreters working upon foundations of assumed certainty, which can, at times, look exceedingly shaky.

***

Historians find ways and means to come to terms with history: it is never simple. Historians have to sort out how they relate to historical material of different types, how they relate to their own past, and how they relate to other people's pasts. Most historians develop their understanding of history through a combination of close and prolonged contact with the material he or she studies, an instinctual reaction to it plus a whole barrage of theory.

As a historian who is also a fiction writer, I must define clearly the sets of relationships that determine my personal or cultural positions towards history. They help me assess for myself in what ways history must be regarded as alien or foreign and what sorts of techniques are called for if I want to move to the level of understanding by which I can interpret history, that is, that cognitive understanding I need as a fiction writer.

To create a level of understanding beyond the Berlitz level, a writer must extract and mine the material from their sources. Rather than mining data and information, they are mining the data and key elements of its context. They must bring at least part of the contexts along, for otherwise the data will be integrated into modern contexts. All of this must be translated into narrative. It then becomes part of the story and helps to make it feel more real to the reader.

Solid research grounds the story. It means that readers know more about the characters and how they live. It also means that the writers can write detail that leads readers into a deeper understanding of the historical background.

If the novel or story has class as an element, the reader is saved extraneous and dull explanation if the writer keys elements that indicate class into the story using telling detail. For instance, how does someone knock on a door? One can explain someone's class status at great length, or one can describe knocking on the door as gentle and ladylike and then have the door open to show a lady and instantly a reader knows that the woman is not a charlady. This is not just being historically accurate and building a solid world for the novel, it is working with the reader's expectations to produce a narrative that is easier to interpret.

A writer can demonstrate the most wonderful intellectual understanding of a subject, but if there is no equivalent emotional understanding then sources are liable to be misinterpreted. It is not a matter of how much research, it's a matter of how much understanding. Why is a detail important? Until a writer reaches this stage, they are liable to assume that all our ancestors were less intelligent than we are or that the past has to be represented with suitably archaic language.

Every writer has to think through these issues. Each has to discover for themselves that a superb intellectual understanding of history is never quite enough for fiction.

The language issue is particularly vexed in fiction: some writers choose to create the feeling of archaic language through invention and reconstruction; some choose to seek more neutral language; some move towards sentence lengths and the shape and feel of the text to create a feel for the period, while some seek specific vocabulary that will precisely illuminate. All of these approaches are ways the writer moves from the intellectual understanding into the place they stand for the successful integration of history into their story.

History provides writers with the information they need and the understanding they require in order to build a sustainable world for the novel. This includes a discussion of the difference between the overview of a place and time, mining a work for cultural tidbits, and mining a work for data. Questions that underpin this are the following:

1) How does this affect the world/story place include how does it enrich it, what questions it poses?
2) How does this affect plot arcs?
3) How does this affect characters and their personal arcs?
4) How does this affect voice?
5) How do writers use this to give the location (place, time) its own character (i.e. make it more real)?

This can be broken down into the writer having a general understanding of their period, into the writer understanding the cultural and political contexts of the time and place they are writing about and into the writer creating a story place. The story itself rests on this story place, but the historical elements of it often consist of data that has been mined and reinterpreted. This data reinforces their intellectual constructs and that reinforcement supports this understanding.

Brian Wainwright demonstrates the mentality involved in this when he explains that experience is important to his use of history in his novels. 'I read a lot of reviews, because if an academic work has flaws, the author's peers are usually quick to spot them and are better qualified to do so than I am. I try to read all sources critically; this applies even to primary sources. I have learned that medieval chroniclers were biased and that medieval clerks often made sloppy mistakes.'

His use of history is active, not passive, and he continually re-evaluates his relationship with the past and with the data he can find about it, in order to transform it into fiction.

Not all world building has realism as its basis. Not all history in fiction is representative of possible or even credible realities. What convincing novels share, therefore, is not necessarily cutting-edge historical scholarship. They share the writer's emotional comprehension of the history that underpins the world of the novel. These writers have developed an emotional affinity with their setting that enables them to convincing devise characters and plots and to tell a story within that setting.

The genre choices an author makes helps shape the world they create for their novel and it also helps shape the way this world is communicated: it is an active participant in creating the typically finite world that most novels require to operate effectively.

This links to the way writers handle the reader/text relationship. Some writers write to specific markets: this is tight genre writing, following the specific tropes and rules for a given genre at a given time. Many romance novels are of this kind, where the reader expects a love interest and for it to be challenged or threatened and then for the challenge or threat to be resolved, for instance. While some genre novels have a tight link with their readers, that is, the novel follows reader expectations for the larger part, not all do. Some types of fantasy fiction, for instance, intentionally break with reader expectations. George R. R. Martin's tendency to kill familiar characters is an example of this.

Thus, for each type of novel, writers are likely to have in their minds a type of reader relationship and this informs their genre choices which in turn informs their world building. How consciously writers use their knowledge of readers to inform their narrative choices is something that warrants further discussion.

Novels are not neutral creations: they are dynamic forces within the cultures in which they operate. They fulfil different roles in culture to history, for the most part, and exceptions to this belong to a different discussion. The different role is related to the nature of the novel. To understand this, however, it is necessary to dig deeply into how novels operate and how writers conceive of history and their own fiction.

CHAPTER 5

The credibility of the story

No matter how much work the writer puts into the understanding of history for their novel, no matter what their research choices are and how they work with those choices, there is a fundamental reality that writers face: they write for audiences. Research and an understanding of history is not what readers see; they see a story set in the world that the writer has created for the novel.

In creating a world for the novel, writers enter story space. That is to say, world building takes them into the story space from which they write the novel. It is quite different to the story space experienced by the reader. Story space is generally discussed as the point at which the reader enters the story, with their assumptions, with their prior knowledge, with their beliefs. Story space for writers overlaps with that of readers, as, in the creation of the story, writers call on many of the same elements readers call on to interpret the novel. Story space for readers has been explored in narratology studies (see Huhn, 2015, for example).

The decisions about what history is going into a novel and how it will be communicated are complex. The essential component is that the reader can be drawn into the narrative. It is not as simple as 'My readers will read the text in this way, therefore this is what I'm going to do.' How 'real' this narrative will feel will depend very much on the type of narrative and the techniques the writer uses to create it. These decisions (that impact the story space of the reader) are placed into the narrative in that other story space, that of the writer. Underlying both is the relationship of the writer with history. In world building and story space, the writer draws on their history to create and interpret the story. This rests heavily on how the writer approaches their research.

Writers seldom articulate their workings in detail. Guy Gavriel Kay (Auden, n.d.) explains that:

> For me, and I suspect for many people who struggle to shape creative works, it [selection of historical details] doesn't take place in so precise a fashion. I can't actually *tell* you how I choose details, or reject them. Sometimes I have a note to use a piece of information and it doesn't get into the book because there isn't room or time, it feels gratuitous, forced, or like one of those raw information dumps I dislike in other people's books (and try, accordingly, to avoid in my own).

Exceptions exist. Kate Grenville's thoughts about her research for *The Secret River* (2006) were published as *Searching for the Secret River* (2008). The memoir explores her journey of exploration in building the world of her novel and in establishing a story space. It is more about her research process and the discovery she made rather than how she wrote once she entered the space of the novel.

In my own novel, *Langue[dot]doc 1305* (2014) I also went on a journey of discovery. I built up an image in my mind of the world of the Languedoc in 1305 using a mixture of primary and secondary sources, studies of social behaviour and mentalities, topographical and geological maps and a careful exploration of the region itself. My intent was to build up a world in which I could tell a story. The story space in my mind was not the whole region, nor the whole period. It was the specific picture I developed for that particular tale.

Readers do not have my vision when they read, for they do not read the sources I used prior to exploring the world of the novel: we thus enter this world from different spaces. Readers' story space is based on their general understanding of the place and period and type of story. Whether their story space is for a historical fiction novel, a time travel novel, or a literary novel depends very much on how they interpret the story itself. My understanding of medieval masculinities or pilgrimage – however carefully developed – is only visible in terms of how it affects the story and the lives of the characters within *Langue[dot]doc 1305*.

Before we can explore these topics, however, some groundwork must be laid. This concerns the credibility of the story and how it fits within current understanding of a period and place. If the writer sets a novel in the

Middle Ages, they need to work with popular conceptions of the Middle Ages as well as those presented by historians. Credibility is not as simple as recounting the 'facts' of the past. It has to meet the tale structure and story type. It is a mediation between the history of historians and the story expectations for a given storytelling framework. If a novel is set in the early nineteenth century, a writer's choices might range from a Heyer-like romantic world or a Napoleonic, grittier tale. Each choice requires a different mediation by the writer. A Heyer-like romance uses witty dialogue and carefully researched clothes, with the research linked to the descriptions formulated by Georgette Heyer, such as sprig muslin worn by young ladies of quality who are 'almost out'. If such a tale deviates too far from the model, the credibility suffers. When some of the structure of a Heyer novel is applied to a novel based on the Napoleonic wars, other devices are often used to shore up the credibility. For example, in Naomi Novik's series about the dragon Temeraire, the fantasy element allows Novik to use Heyer-like dialogue without compromising the credibility.

A narrative that rests on a series of popular images of the Middle Ages will find its emotional resonance more easily than one that draws upon a scholarly Middle Ages, for example, as the pageant and the emotional validation in history tend to come from popular narratives, reinforced through cultural sharing. Felicity Pulman's *I, Morgana* (2014) – where the plot is drawn directly from popular Arthurian narratives from Malory onwards – is quite different to her Janna series, where she relies more on the scholarly interpretation of the Middle Ages. The credibility of each narrative does not depend on the quite different use of history within each. The higher level of concordance with a historian's view of the Middle Ages in the Janna novels reflects the higher level of realism in detective and coming-of-age novels, while the credibility of Morgana relies on different factors such as the exploration of familiar Arthurian motifs and stories.

The genre choices of the author are critical to the successful mediation of factors that creates credibility of the history in fiction. The light, romanticized fiction of Heyer herself in her lighter Regency novels (such as *Bath Tangle* [1955] or *Regency Buck* [1935]), where the main intent is humorous flirtation/romance, can usefully be compared with Bernard Cornwell's Sharpe series. Each set of stories is grounded on a different interpretation of history by the writer and formed into a narrative and genre that suit those choices. Heyer's prose is light and witty, whereas Cornwell's is full of action and moral uncertainty.

From a writer's point of view, narratives can be roughly divided into those that are probable, improbable, or plausible:

1. Are probable

Probable narratives take the historical narratives and data about the past and interpret them in a way that falls close enough to the way historians explain the period that it is possible to say 'It's not history, but it could have happened that way'. Currently, this approach has strong cultural currency. A recent example of this is Hilary Mantel's *Wolf Hall* (2010), the cultural currency of which can be clearly seen in its Booker win. Of the interviewees, Elizabeth Chadwick's historical fiction and Brian Wainwright's historical fiction create probable fiction (although not, it must be noted, Wainwright's comic fiction. Wainwright's comic fiction is not under study here and Wainwright's answers to questions were given specifically in relation to his serious historical fiction).

Works that fit into this probable category are more likely to represent the historical fiction aspect of genre: the narrative choices of historical fiction writers are frequently closer to the choices of a narrative historian than the choices of a speculative fiction writer. It is not what happened. It is not a precise representation of what we believe to have happened (that is to say, it is not close to standard historical narratives about that place and time) but it can come quite close to this in popular narrative terms. On the whole they seek more accurate representation of the past, which, in reality, means they seek a narrative that is as close as possible to the modern educated interpretation of that past era. The 'probable' are the closest to the historian's choices of narrative style where the historian chooses a linear narrative, such as when they chronicle the sequential events of the life of a historic person.

2. Are improbable

When narrative choices are made with less sense of the modern educated interpretation of the past era, then the bundling of these choices creates a novel that is read as improbable rather than probable. Quite simply, the writer is not narrating a past that is to be trusted historically. This approach may have either or both of artistic merit and audience appeal, but it has little connection to history.

The work of Kathleen Woodiwiss, for instance, focuses so much on the narrative conventions of romance and uses such a Berlitz notion of the historical background that it meets up with standard historical narrative at very few points. She gives a clear indication of this in her use of such narrative devices as the dialogue style that Dave Luckett describes as 'Forsoothly'. 'What cruel twist of fate that I be born beneath the blighting branches of my father's wealth,' declares the heroine in the opening pages of *Shanna* (2009). The colour and idiom add to the romantic feel (for it is a narrative convention very typical of old-fashioned historical romances) while contradicting the current historical understanding of language use. Comparing this choice of dialogue with that of a writer who works closer to received history, Elizabeth Chadwick explains in her interview that she uses the closest to neutral language she can find when she writes dialogue, specifically to avoid the sense of false dating. Neutral language, for instance, avoids distinctively modern words such as 'OK' and intentional archaisms such as 'Forsooth.' Thus an awareness of the narrative conventions and how they relate to the historical conventions can push a specific work further away from the improbable and towards the probable.

Some novels appear entirely *impossible* from the point of known history. They contain events which cannot happen; exotic beings are created, or physics does not operate as we believe it should. Paranormal historical romances with their vampires and werewolves are an excellent example of a whole branch of novels that do not fit our current perceptions of reality. For this branch of novels, which includes a wide range of work ranging from those paranormal romances to William Mayne's *Earthfasts* (1995) and

Roberta MacAvoy's *The Book of Kells* (1985), the question is much simpler: are they credible? Can the reader suspend their disbelief and move through the story able to temporarily trust in its reality?

3. Are plausible

Somewhere between probable and improbable lie the works of most fiction writers. Works which are probable are the closest to the narratives of historians' choices. Works which are improbable have no similar overlap with the choices of historians. Neither grouping, however, typifies *genre fiction* that uses history. The vast majority of genre fiction is simply *plausible*. Events may or may not have happened, the people may or may not have lived, but within the novel they are part of an effective narrative. The writer has convinced the reader that the novel is sustainable but has not created a historically credible world for the novel – that is to say, the events and interpretations in the novel can easily be compared against current historical narratives and found to be fictional. This is when the setting is plausible, but unlikely to represent historical reality as the readers (especially historically trained readers) see it.

When a story is *plausible*, it is not a precise representation of what we believe happened, but it has clear indications that it cannot have happened within known history. The writer still, however, creates a credible story. When magic is introduced into a narrative, for example, or known events peopled with invented characters, these can be clear indications that a sequence of events is expected to be considered as plausible rather than probable.

These three categories distinguish between narratives that are closely linked to the historical narratives of historians, and those that have larger elements of invention or of reliance on popular narratives. The events may or may not have happened, the people may or may not have lived, but they give (to varying degrees) the impression that they did.

***

One of the most significant differences between popular history and the work of historians is the prevalence of popular misconceptions about a place and time. These popular misconceptions push many works of fiction from the probable to the plausible or even to the improbable end of the spectrum. Examples of this include Michael Crichton's misuse of polyglottal speech in *Timeline*, for instance, or Kim Stanley Robinson's assumption in *Galileo's Dream* that the Middle Ages was a period typified by stupidity, or the lack of cleanliness observed in dining by the Jewish protagonist in the opening sequences of Bryce Courtney's *The Potato Factory*. Crichton's first swordplay scene in *Timeline* is quite different in its effect to his use of language by characters. Marek, the novel's protagonist, is built up as plausible as he is demonstrably (through his recreational activities) a research student with special expertise in swordplay.

This demonstrates the complexity of the roles history plays in fiction. Writers do not create simple realities. Some elements of their work may be more deeply thought out or more effective on the probability scale than others. Different readers may judge the novel based on different elements and come to quite disparate conclusions concerning the plausibility or other of a given narrative.

Popular misconceptions and popular assumptions are quite different strands of narrative concerning the past. Where a story is intended to reinforce a particular thread it will accept assumptions and misconceptions that reinforce that thread. Where a story is not so accepting, it will be closer to the constant reinterpretation of historians: a good example is Josephine Tey's *The Daughter of Time*, where the protagonist is a detective who professionally questions More's account of the story of Richard III and tries to tell his own more accurate version.

One of the most significant questions facing fiction writers with an historical base to their novels is how to deal with their existing assumptions and in particular with popular misconceptions concerning a period. There are two key problem-areas that writers must address.

The first of these lies in the situation where the writer's own assumptions overshadow historical interpretation to such a degree that they colour it quite differently and present a view of a period that appears problematic when compared to historical accounts. This is when the world a writer depicts is significantly different from the same time and place as explained by historians. For example, This in Connie Willis' time-travel novel *To Say Nothing of the Dog* (1997), the main characters travel back to an England that is clearly the England of Jerome K. Jerome's comic writings, to a large extent re-enacting Jerome's 1859 novel *Three Men in a Boat* as a quest-adventure. It describes a fictional England created by someone else as if it were a real past: this shows off the literary artifice that is the built world. The world building of the novelist creates a complex and exquisite artifice that is essential to the story being told. The literary references in Willis' books serve as a useful reminder that the primary function of novels is to tell stories, not to explain the past.

The second problem-area lies in the potential assumptions readers may bring to their interpretation of a given novel. This is a more difficult area. A writer cannot know what assumptions any given reader may hold, although it is reasonable to assume that many readers will hold popular misconceptions.

The writer may share the popular misconceptions with potential readers, and may choose to narrate using them as a base. They may also address these misconceptions using references to scholars to develop a new understanding of a place and time, one that matches more closely with cutting edge research by historians. This is a greater problem for some historical settings than others – for example, misconceptions concerning the Middle Ages are so prevalent and appear so often in popular culture that a group of Medievalists placed an online volume addressing some of them on Orb, a popular reference website for Medieval Europe (Harris and Grigsby, 2001).

Writers have different techniques for handling their assumptions. Some alert the reader that they hold those assumptions. Willis does this in her *Doomsday Book* when she develops characters who make gross errors of judgement concerning the period: this is an alert that real history and fictional history only overlap to a degree. The difficulty with Willis' approach is that it also makes modern scholars look abysmally ignorant of the subject in which they are specialists. In pushing the reader's trust and judgement onto the narrator, Willis endangers the reader's perception of the reliability of the historical knowledge of scholars. This boundary issue suggests that the handling of one's prior knowledge of a period is fundamental to fiction that uses history.

Other writers add an author's note to their novel. Isolde Martyn, for example, appends a 'History Note' to *The Lady and the Unicorn* (1998). In just over a page (1998: 355–56) Martyn presents an overview of what is known about the major characters and the state of source material concerning them. These additions to the novel-proper enable the reader to form their own judgements concerning reliability by giving them the tools to assess the writer's research.

A bibliography or author's note, however, may also be intended by the author to shift them along the probability scale and to be associated with a higher level of historical awareness in the reader's mind. This latter can be seen in Michael Crichton's bibliography for *Timeline*. It does not address any of the issues of interpretation of history within the novel, but it makes a clear statement that the novel has been carefully researched. This demonstrates that it is not the level or quantity of data established through research, necessarily, that determines a work's place on the credibility scale, but how cannily the research is undertaken by the author and how much they question their own assumptions concerning that period of history.

Another approach is to create a fantasy history. By de-linking from our own perceptions of our past through adding fantastical elements, the writer indicates that the history has imaginary elements. An example already mentioned is Paul McAuley's *Pasquale's Angel*, however Chaz Brenchley's *Hand of the King's Evil* (2002) decouples even further by creating a world that has similar history to ours but also has fantastical elements such as djinns (just as McAuley creates a fantastical Renaissance Italy) but changes most of the common names and places. This de-linking moves a story away from history as we receive it and an impossible narrative is created. Its credibility as a story is more important than its probability.

Not only are there many approaches, the views of authors on the subject express the individuality inherent in the choice of approach. Some joke about it, as Michael Barry did when, in the 2004–5 interviews, he was asked about his interaction with non-academic subject experts and replied: 'I have little interaction with such people. I dread infection.' Others see their role as avoiding mistakes, but imply that some are inevitable. Kathleen Cunningham

Guler explains this when she says that 'Most readers (unfortunately) would never know the difference [on historical detail] ... but there will always be one out there that has to rake the author over the coals for a mistake, no matter how minor.' Sophie Masson sums up why authors choose to diverge from the work of historians and why many writers do not question all elements that, perhaps, historians would question when she explains that 'You can't become a prisoner of your source material or your novel dies'; Helen Hollick says simply '*No* historical fiction book can, by its very nature, be totally accurate'.

Nevertheless, writers may question assumptions about received history. Debra Kemp does this while discussing research she did in developing her key character, a female knight named Grisandole: 'there is precedence for a female knight in the Vulgate cycle. Grisandole, you go, girl!'

Popular knowledge of history has its own culture. These views by writers help explain how that culture develops.

***

The belief the reader has in the story while in their (the reader's) story space is vital. It is very important to note that it is not the same as facts (whether a given historical event happened on this day or on another) or as verisimilitude. Facts and verisimilitude can assist with credibility, but so can strong characterization or a believable plot. This history used by a writer in a novel is only one facet of credibility.

The issue with credibility is that writers may be tempted to *invent*, rather than *build* using current historical understanding. That is, they move further away from current historical narratives than the story requires. Sometimes this results in gorgeously exotic worlds (in the work of Guy Gavriel Kay, for instance) where the writer has been clever enough to create an otherworld narrative, one that feels historical through clever links with known historical places and time. In his 1992 work *A Song for Arbonne*, Kay works with a purpose-built region that is linked strongly to the south of France and in an invented time that roughly parallels the Albigensian Crusade and its aftermath. By creating significant ties with the history of our thirteenth-century France and bringing both popular narratives and historical narratives concerning the region into the novel, Kay creates a plausible novel. It is not real, but it is deeply credible.

The credibility of the history presented and that of the novel itself are very important in evaluating the use of history in speculative fiction, because this genre suffers potential loss of credibility in always situating itself in the vicinity of the unknown. Its 'What if?' assumptions immediately take the reader away from the reality they know. This affects the use of history in science fiction and fantasy because, as we have seen, what looks probable in fictional narratives draws its capacity to convince from its nearness to other narratives, whether they be those of scholarly history or those of popular history. Speculative fiction intends (at least in theory) to create credible narratives while breaking with these other narratives, the result of the 'What if?' equation that lies at its heart.

Speculative fiction writers still have a range of decisions to make, however, from reinforcing the reality of the strange past (as Harry Turtledove does in his alternate history, by providing a significant amount of historical detail and telling detail in the openings to his novels, to help the reader situate themselves, or as Joan Aiken does in her Wolves of Willoughby Chase alternate fantasy history, where she uses the modern views of the grime and cruelty of the Industrial Revolution for the same end) or to creating whole new worlds, based on material they know from our world (as the Rohirrim in J. R. R. Tolkien's *Lord of the Rings* series have some very close parallels with the culture and society of early medieval England) or they can choose mythic or literary models (Gene Wolfe's *The Devil in the Forest*, for instance, creates a medieval fantasy village). This range of choices is possible because, as David N. Samuelson says (1993: 192), the symbolic capital of science fiction derives from the importance of the hypothetical, that it is 'a model of something not yet known, theoretically possible, but beyond human experience'.

In other words, while the reality of the story still has to be communicated to the reader, the ways that credibility of the history in the story can be achieved are flexible. This is explained by Lisa Yaszek (2009: 198) when she discusses the philosophy of history in science fiction studies. She points out that science fiction is 'a compelling vehicle for the expression of modern social values'. This enables that wider choice of tools to achieve credibility and, at the same time, it opens up the genre to historically based novels by writers such as Kurt Vonnegut and Joanna Russ, novels that experiment with our sense of history and that, in fact, are able to test that sense.

Genre, therefore is important to the reader, and so are genre indicators. Whether a novel is historical fiction or historical fantasy matters,
the genre signals how to interpret the history within the story, whether
a scale of probability will work in terms of assessing it, or whether credibility is more important. It helps the reader establish what aspects of the
history in the novel are to be treated as trustworthy. Using a particular
genre underpins the credibility of the historical aspects of a novel, and
provides the stylistic tools the writer can use to shore up or undermine
that credibility.

Some of the tools that a writer may use to increase the credibility of
their narrative include *spectacle, telling detail* and *character interaction*:

Spectacle

Spectacle is an important aspect of most genre fiction. The type of spectacle
varies according to the genre. In some cases it is description: in historical
fiction novels, for instance, an army is likely to be described in detail to give
it that sense of spectacle. In historical fantasy action is often important.
Dave Luckett's 1998 fantasy novel *A Dark Winter* contains much military
action, for example, as it is a story concerning saving the castle of Ys from
the armies of the Dark. The military element is so critical to the tale that
there are pictures of weapons and armour after the map in the front matter.

Spectacle helps to convince the reader that the narrative is solid and
thus that the research underlying the narrative is sufficient; that is, it reinforces the credibility of the narrative. It is not sufficient for the reader if
the novelist is educated in science: the novel itself must play with science
in an acceptable way to convince the reader.

A fantasy country needs to have certain tropes to indicate that it is
based on an acceptable understanding of the Middle Ages: knights, religious persecution, belief in magic, nobles, monks, long dresses and suffering
peasants are all used by a range of writers to establish credibility. Spectacle

is an essential element of genre novels and links the reader with their literary assumptions concerning a place and time. This is how it shores up credibility without necessarily linking the novel closely to known history.

Spectacle can be seen, perhaps, as elements culturally linked to the public perception of the history of a place and time that can be used to establish an emotional link with that place and time. These elements do not necessarily reflect deeper truths about the past and some, such as chastity belts, may be modern inventions associated with that place and time (in this case the Middle Ages) through popular culture with the links made stronger through their attraction for popular culture.

Telling detail

'Telling detail' is a phrase most often use by historical fiction writers to describe a small piece of information that indicates a great deal of other material to the reader. A good example of telling detail is in Roberta MacAvoy's *The Book of Kells* (1985). Two characters have a conversation about how many bowls are needed for the table (1985: 176). This conversation not only shows the relationship between the two characters, but it also demonstrates the significant differences in culture between the modern and the early medieval characters, for it demonstrates differences between how meals are taken.

Character interaction

Another interesting tool is the use of interaction between characters to enhance the credibility of the narrative through presenting historical information. The reader needs to know this information in order to interpret the story in such a way that it becomes intrinsic to the narrative. The historical information, however, is equally necessary to establish characters and to advance the plot. For example, in Felicity Pulman's *Rosemary for Remembrance* (2005: 11) a self-important healer called Fulk tries to get help with a case that is beyond his ability. Pulman uses our modern (very limited) knowledge of medieval medicine at the village level in the scene but the credibility is attained through the characters' interactions with each other.

The character interaction is far more comfortable for modern readers than a presentation of theoretical information about the nature of medical understanding in the Middle Ages, and it is this comfort rather than the detail of the medical situation itself that provides the level of verisimilitude. However, if the medical situation were absurd to modern readers or lacked the sense that Pulman had researched properly, then even the situational credibility would have been undermined.

That the narrative choices and character interaction are just as much a part of historical credibility as historical research is reinforced in Alison Uttley's *A Traveller in Time* when we see that her historical explanations are often couched in conversations. She does not treat them as neutral – they help establish how the reader sees the past through the eyes of the characters; for example, when Phoebe Drury says that she has seen shops on London Bridge, the note of faint boastfulness and wonder in her comment effectively supplies the context and support of the historical place and time. (1977: 125)

To achieve credibility, therefore, a fiction writer uses the devices they need within their particular genre to convince the reader of the power of their story. In heroic fantasy with a historical flavour (such as that of George R. R. Martin or Joe Abercrombie), the main tools used are characterization, pageant/spectacle, tension, emotional manipulation. In addition, they link other narratives and those narratives are often historical and thus they reinforce the sense of history within the novel without having to be as precise about the history they are reflecting. For example, the first volume of Martin's *A Song of Ice And Fire* contains many sequences that reflect the chronicles of the later Middle Ages, and Joe Abercrombie in *The Heroes* recreates a popular view of the Napoleonic wars. In Martin's case, his historicity and apparent historical flavour uses such a wide range of tools that the reader's attention is drawn away from the fact that his societies are entirely unsustainable. He writes the story of suffering and handles it so very well (through the pageant and through the characterization) that the reader believes in it. History doesn't have to be accurate: societies don't have to be able to feed themselves or have viable justice or communication systems.

***

The relationship between scholarship, popular assumptions and fictional history is complex. Intrinsic to it is the ways the past and history are mediated and presented to us. This is a deeply studied area, but scholarship has been largely confined to examining published works and established writers. The 2004–5 interviews I conducted help ascertain just how a group of authors feel as part of that mediation and interpret what they were doing when they were writing history into fiction. One aim of the questions was to find out what view of history (and in particular of the Middle Ages) authors of genre fiction brought to their work while working on it. As is becoming obvious, there are significant differences when one examines the writers' interface with the past. Where the focus is on the work, clear techniques emerge and those techniques follow genre lines to achieve credibility within those lines. When the focus is returned to the writers, however, lines become blurred.

All of the writers interviewed are passionate about history. Whether that history is written as probable or plausible or pure fantasy, however, depends on the writer and on how they see research, and to a certain extent on how the writer defines what they are writing. The writers' responses demonstrated a deep commitment to writing and narrative, and the part that history played in that depended very much on the writer's personality and genre definition. Fiction is, for these writers, an individual statement and something very personal. Elizabeth Chadwick said it most succinctly: 'I write what I personally want to write. I'm fortunate in that readers want to read it! If ever I lost my publishing contract I might have to think of writing something else, but it would be just a job than a passion.'

There is a fundamental difference between writers' relationship with history, not according to what they have studied or where they were brought up, but according to what genre they associate with. This was visible in the choice of writing techniques examined earlier, but is also clear from the interview responses.

The fantasy writers and writers who have a speculative fiction base in general (such as Dave Luckett and Michael Barry) are much less concerned with aligning their fiction with the probable. When Dave Luckett describes himself as 'not caring a toss', he is suggesting that the internal consistency of the novel and the world of the novel is far more important than its relationship with known history.

These narrative choices are closely linked to how individual writers approach the research for the novel.

One issue was the use of consultation with others who are experts in the field. Elizabeth Chadwick, representing the historical fiction side, consults where she can. She provides a list of Medievalists she has consulted with (Crouch, Burgess and myself). She checks her research with each scholar rather than asking preliminary questions. For instance, on a question concerning the twelfth/thirteenth-century leader William Marshal, 'Professor Crouch couldn't answer my question because he couldn't answer it himself – which was useful since if the foremost authority on William Marshal doesn't know the answer, I'm not likely to get many letters of complaint if I choose the wrong date for William's brother's marriage.' She uses professional historians, therefore, to check the limits of her knowledge, to describe the boundaries in which she can work, and to know where invention is possible because the lack of historical record permits it. She is writing alongside the historical narrative of historians and uses their work to help her maintain that link. Her writing is intentionally probable rather than plausible. She attains the credibility within her fiction through working with standard historical narratives offered by historians. The checks she makes with historians are crucial to understanding her work.

Another writer who works clearly within historical fiction and works alongside scholarly history is Brain Wainwright. He explains that:

> Medievalists are particularly helpful in explaining arcane procedures – enfeoffments for example. It's rare that they can help with developing the personality of a character because they don't usually have enough intimate personal detail to satisfy a novelist. The issues that are significant to a professional historian are not necessarily those that

float the boat of a fiction writer and vice versa. It is interesting that some academics – no names, no packdrill – can be more speculative about controversial events than a novelist would dare to be!

This demonstrates a different type of boundary. No matter how close a novelist comes to the historical narratives of historians, there will always be differences. The written narratives are different in form and intent. Wainwright illuminates this difference. When a historian moves into the ground that Wainwright defines as that of the novelist ('developing the personality of a character') it creates a porous boundary between fiction and history. Ann Wroe's work on the nature of a medieval French town as expressed through its legal system, *A Fool and His Money: Life in a Partitioned Town in Fourteenth Century France* (1995), enters this terrain. While this is not key to understanding how fiction writers use history, an understanding that the boundary is porous and can be crossed from the historian's side helps us understand that Wainwright's definition is of his own work and of his own perception of the difference between history and fiction. The development of characters through carefully observed minute detail about their lives is typical of his novel *Within the Fetterlock*: his observations are critical to understanding that he is carefully positioning this novel on the probable end of the spectrum, but that it is, in his mind, still fictional and still contains a significant element of invention. He is not writing history: he is writing fiction.

Catherine Butler developed a working relationship for the purposes of researching fiction. She explains when interviewed: 'My academic helper has indeed been helpful. He told me various things about medieval local politics and the personalities involved, the dates at which judicial torture was used (officially or otherwise), the laws against witchcraft, and so on, that might (had I not known them) have led me to put chronologically incompatible features into the book – although luckily these were relatively easy to fix. (Public events don't play a large role in my book.)' This reinforces the statements by Wainwright and Chadwick.

Felicity Pulman gives the last of the really interesting answers in this category. She explains that most of her help has not been from historians. Nevertheless, she has the same approach to finding information from people as the earlier writers:

In my experience, everyone I've ever asked for information has been more than happy to share his/her knowledge with me. I've really appreciated their time and their patience in answering my questions. Occasionally they'll misunderstand what I need to know, or will go off the track on some particular passion of their own. While this can be somewhat time-wasting, you sometimes get unexpected information which can really add depth or colour to a story. I've learned it pays to be prepared with questions and to make sure they answer them all, no matter how fascinating the other stuff might be. And I've learned to listen for those unexpected nuggets which so often make all the difference.

The importance in this is how she uses her received information; how it is translated into story.

Story underpins the questions asked of experts and when the experts questioned do not realize this, crossed-wires may ensue. Tamara Mazzei explains this most explicitly:

Even if they were more approachable, experts don't seem to understand that it isn't feasible to check a long list of references for evidence of the existence (or lack thereof) of a single item when it may take months, or even years to get hold of the recommended sources – the case for many who aren't connected with academia.

I've also noticed that if there isn't evidence 'for' something, it appears that means I'm not supposed to use it. Yet, the main reason I would consult an expert is because I'm not sure about something I already wish to use. I'm not looking for a reason 'to' use it; I'm looking for reasons why I shouldn't.

For example, if I were to receive an answer like this: 'it wasn't introduced until the seventeenth century' then that is a reason not to use something and I wouldn't use it. On the other hand, I interpret a reply like this: 'it was known in the Middle Ages, but there is no evidence that it was in use that early' as an argument 'for' using something because the first evidence for use might not be the earliest actual use – it may only be the earliest surviving evidence.

Not all writers seek expert advice, however, or seek it at the same stage in their work. These writers are less likely to be writing to achieve a probable past. For them, plausibility is sufficient. Michael Barry sums up the approach of this group when he explains that he has no interaction with subject experts, although he might ask one as an expert reader, late in the proceedings.

What writers suggest in their approach to historians is that they focus their questions quite clearly and that the nature of their novel is important. Adding this to the earlier conclusions, it seems probable that the plot/character dominates and is critical to more writers, but that the historical fiction writers will attach themselves more closely to the expected historical narratives as established by known historians.

Part of the historical debate is how much one can know about the past and how much of our understanding is layer upon layer of interpretation – that is, upon narratives about the past, explaining it and interpreting it. Georg Lukács argues that the language of reality is 'personal, participant, and historical' (cited in Malvasi and Nelson, 2005: xiv). The writing of history into anything always exceeds the empirical (Alun Munslow explores this for the writing of history) and always contains culturally relative and narrative interpretative elements. The novelist's negotiations of a relationship with scholars of history and, more importantly, with other historical narratives, are critical in helping place their work along the various axes discussed here. The role of the fiction writer in engaging with history is no less 'personal, participant and historical' than the role of others who develop narratives concerning the past.

Narratives created by historians entail choices. Hayden White includes arranging events, answering questions, including, excluding, stressing or focussing on particular areas in these choices in *Metahistory*. Narratives are not neutral. Writers make these choices all the time. The evidence of their choices is less in the interaction with experts than with the narrative choices they make for their novels. Through these tools, we can understand the individuality of each writer and the decisions they make that orient them in terms of credibility and verisimilitude.

Mink (1970: 545) points out that 'An historical narrative does not demonstrate the necessity of events but makes them intelligible by unfolding the story which connects their significance.' He then suggests that history 'is obligated to rest upon evidence of the occurrence in real space and time' and grows out of critical assessment of received materials. This demonstrates quite nicely the relationship between credibility (reader's faith in the narrative, whether fact-based or invented), the facts (the stuff upon which historical interpretation must rest, but which is not as essential or fiction writers) and verisimilitude.

Placing this into more normative historiographical discourse, Lion Feuchtwanger (1935) sums up the most common argument for historical facts as a source of credibility in fiction when he says, 'I have always made an effort to render every detail of my reality with the greatest accuracy; but I have never paid attention to whether my presentation of historical facts was an exact one. Indeed, I have often altered evidence which I knew to be documented if it appeared to interfere with my intended effect.'

Chaz Brenchley, when interviewed, suggests that a writer's responsibility to maintain historical accuracy varies:

> If as I do they're mapping historical themes into secondary-world fiction, then the question really doesn't apply; the history of this planet may be echoed on another world, but it's not going to be replicated. If they're writing real-world historical fiction, the obviously it's an issue … it's all about interpretation, and every writer gets to choose for themselves how much or how little they stick to what is known. Sometimes it's fun to use the facts within the narrative (the way Neal Stephenson does e.g.: if a couple of historical characters are known to have died of smallpox, why not have a fictional character give it to them? Deliberately …?); sometimes the facts just get in the way of a good story, at which point it's the writer's choice every time. There is no responsibility to history, only to the story, to make it the best you can. For some writers, that means adhering close to the track of history; for some it means dancing away.

Modern writers of historical fiction, in particular, are more reluctant to alter known history, as we have seen in the careful discussion made by both Wainwright and Chadwick concerning how to situate their stories in relationship to what is 'known' about history.

If the fiction writer doesn't base their story on evidence or is willing to change the evidence, however, then verisimilitude must be achieved in the actual telling of the tale. Mary Stewart creates verisimilitude for a place and time for which little evidence exists by clearly linking to Geoffrey of Monmouth in her Crystal Cave sequence of novels. The authority of Geoffrey creates the verisimilitude and the fact that he is not contemporaneous with her late Romano-British narrative is immaterial. The links are made in the afterword and the reflection of Geoffrey's very short tale in a work of four volumes creates a sense of historical truth where virtually none exists in terms of political timelines and events.

More recently, supplementary material might be included on a website. For instance, Ekaterina Sedia adds to the cultural value of her fiction by adding to the verisimilitude of the novel outside it; that is to say, she uses her website. This is not scholarly apparatus. The explanations and bibliographies included in these notes shores up the reader's belief in the story. It's all about the reader.

When credibility fails (as it does for Lukács on reading Tom Wolfe's *Bonfire of the Vanities*, 2005: 338–48) it fails because the writer has set his goals too high (for Lukács as a reader of Wolfe's work, the novel is set up as more than fiction and fails to deliver on this credibly) or has genre indications that are not met (for example, in Crichton's *Timeline*, where it is set up as science fiction and gives a bibliography, but has levels of fact and accuracy more suited to a thriller). This loss of audience belief also happens, however, when historical narratives are different, when different groups see the past in different ways. For instance, William Rainbolt experienced a failure in the credibility of a reader when a reader claimed his novel *Moses Rose* was wrong: ' ... you really changed the history of what actually happened' (n.d.). History itself relies on credibility for acceptance of a particular account, and even factually accurate material has passed the judgement of the readers. Writing techniques and popular assumptions about a place and time are, therefore, just as important to the credibility of a novel as the accuracy of the historical facts.

The use of a reliable observer by Crichton illustrates how very important our perception of a given period is to these issues. The Middle Ages has been particularly well studied in this regard. Trigg (2009) indicates that this is partly due to convergence culture. We own the Middle Ages in various ways and shape our narratives concerning it because of this perceived identity it has. The perceived Middle Ages in Crichton is the location in time of much of the plot, but it is also the professional concern of some of the characters and the recreational concern of at least one other. To achieve credibility for a narration concerning this period, popular perceptions of it have to be addressed, whether or not they are accurate.

As we have seen, the nature of a particular novel is critical to this. Jerome de Groot (2010: 11) suggests that some European novels 'use historical form to reflect on contemporary literature'. The narrative objectives of the novel are part of how the novel achieves its credibility and thus the nature and level of historical verisimilitude necessary. Tosh (2008: 26) explains that 'The foundation of all historical awareness is the recognition that the past is another world.' The fictional past helps us to test that world in our mind. It provides bricks in the wall of our understanding.

When postmodernism deconstructs the divide between high art and mass culture it addresses this issue: what types of narrative validate our experience. In Tosh's words, why does history matter? How do stories matter? These are linked very closely within the novel. All of these options, in other words, take place within the confines of the world of the novel (not the real world) and within the plot of the novel.

What writers do is make choices that work for their novels or for their perception of the world their novel requires in order to function properly within its genre constraints. How a given particular work achieves its credibility depends very much on those genre constraints. In a fantasy novel where the universe operates differently to our universe then the writer assumes that the reader's disbelief will be more easily suspended on most historical matters. In a world that purports to be ours, with our history, the closer to probable the choice is, the larger the number of readers who will be thrown out by large departures from existing popular historical narratives.

There is one significant caveat that must be made. While this popular history generally has a strong relationship with the histories of historians, it is not exactly the same. Some options that are probable, historically, are actually not credible within the confines of fiction. For example (this examples is drawn from student reactions within classroom teaching) while it is technically quite correct to call someone with fair hair a blonde in relationship to the Medieval West, some readers will object to this as anachronistic, for 'blonde' is often regarded as a modern term with modern connotations. Therefore, while it is completely probable that a fair haired woman could be called a blonde in thirteenth-century France, it is not credible for many readers, for their associations with the word outweigh the historical realities.

All decisions a writer makes concerning the use of history are underpinned by the question 'Is this credible?' This credibility is dynamic and partly dependent on popular models of periods and times as much as on the author's reading of scholarly history. The closer a writer can come to 'probable' in relation to the historian's understanding, the more the work will satisfy readers with strong historical backgrounds. Furthermore, the more credible it is, the more it adds to the symbolic capital of the novel. However, novels that use popular assumptions concerning a period (Dan Brown's *The Da Vinci Code*, for example, relies very heavily on the popular fictions espoused in such books as *Holy Blood, Holy Grail*) rely on their entertainment value far more heavily than their historical credibility. It is not simply a matter of cultural capital: it is what type of cultural capital a writer draws on using different approaches to history in their fiction.

Trigg (2008: 109) suggests that 'the patron enhances his own cultural capital' through associating with experts. The writer is changing the cultural value of the reading experience through changing the level of credibility in the novel. This is how the audience enters into the decisions a writer makes concerning history in their fiction, even if a particular writer is not aware of it: by writing for a specific audience, each writer is making choices regarding the need for probable, possible or impossible history, relating to credibility and to popularity. These choices are critical.

CHAPTER 6

Developing the story

Four factors account for key differences between the fiction narrative and the non-fiction narrative. These factors accomplish the task of integrating historical detail into the historian's narrative. The factors are:

1) the quality and focus of the *research*, including sources
2) approaches to and methods of *interpretation* of historical data, how we shape our understanding of the past
3) *responsibility* to present the past accurately
4) *transparency* of the process, including the critical apparatus and other aspects of the text that enable the reader to track the writer's reasoning.

Writers' handling of these factors determines their choices in building the world of their novel.

1. Research

Research for a historian is the process of investigating sources (primary, secondary and other sources such as landscape and archaeological finds). The intent of historians varies according to the style of history they are researching. Thus the research itself entails consulting a range of sources using a range of methods and then the translation from research into writing varies according to the genre the historian works with. An anthropological history or an ethnohistory (such as E. Le Roy Ladurie's *Montaillou* [1981]) is quite different in final form to a more standard politico-social approach (such as James Given's *Inquisition and Medieval Society: Power, Discipline, and Resistance in Languedoc* [1997]). They do, however, both assume a strong relationship with primary sources and both assume that the reader will be able to reconstruct their argument from those sources if they go to the sources.

This is the big difference between research for history and research for fiction. A published novel is generally considered to be an integral narrative because of its status as art. While there is certainly an integral work in a scholarly history and while some scholarly history may be regarded as art (notably Edward Gibbon's *The History of the Decline and Fall of the Roman Empire*), the argument based upon the research is more important than its artistic form. The sources and the argument do not make the core of the work in the novel, whereas they are critical in a history. The role of the writer in interpreting the research is critical and produces an object that is more art that history or, if more carefully researched, at the very least as much art as history. While the expectation is there in all academic histories that the research trail can and ought to be reconstructed and evaluated, it is not there for fiction. In fact, one of the reasons writers are attracted to history in their fiction, as we have seen, is because they can emotionally connect with parts of history that cannot be formally reconstructed. The test of the novel does not rely on the quality of its research, in other words, but in the quality of its craft. Research for a novel has a specific role, therefore. Its chief aim is to enhance the story. Validation of a theoretical argument is secondary, if it exists at all.

2. Interpretation

It is not the act of research that is the critical difference between the work of the historian and the work of the writer who uses history in their fiction: it is the act of interpretation. For the fiction writer, it is not a simple matter of communicating what has been researched and understood. The material is interpreted (that is, transformed) to meet the needs of the story.

Material researched might advance the plot, or aid characterization, or assist in creating credible setting, but it also helps in other matters. For instance, clothes often have a symbolic function in the works of George R. R. Martin, reflecting the drama of the moment or the nature of the character rather than reflecting anything underpinned by solid research. In *Game of Thrones* (1998, 2) Ser Waymer Royle wears black leather boots, black woollen pants, black moleskin gloves and 'a fine supple cloak of gleaming black' ringmail over layers of black wool and boiled leather and (1998: 3) 'His cloak was his crowning glory: sable, thick and black and soft as sin.' The outer layer of cloth is missing. This is critical in armour terms – that is, the item that is missing was one aspect of the defensive element of clothing as it would have been worn in the fourteenth century. The mail is more visually impressive to the modern eye as the outer layer, however, than a tunic would be. The description is given to present a character emotionally, not to describe a historical garment. Likewise, the fur being on the outside indicates that the garments are new, for fur exposed to the elements does not retain that pristine air for long. With this costume, Martin creates a *moment of drama*, not a reality. Interpretation of the moment changes the everyday into the pageant, but it plays with the historical.

3. Responsibility

Writers of fiction have cultural and ethical responsibilities towards the history they use in their fiction. While the historian's responsibility to narrative history has been enunciated and argued for over two centuries (history ethics comprising a significant element of historiography) the responsibility of the novelist towards the past is less discussed. The discussions that have taken place by scholars such as Hayden White, Roland Barthes and Michel Foucault seldom analyse genre novels. While recent discussion by Australian writers such as Kate Grenville (in her work on *The Secret River*, 2006) and Inga Clendinnen (1996, 2006) touch on these issues, they simplify the issues and do not explain the earlier approaches by scholars such as White, nor do they account for the work on the subject by ethnohistorians such as Greg Dening (1988). Tom Griffiths (2009) has begun to reconcile this gap in applying theory and ethics of history to fiction, but the issues are not yet resolved. The central place for current discussion on this subject is taking place in the journal *Rethinking History*.

Genre need and historiographical responsibilities can conflict, as has earlier been suggested. The work of the historian is not the work of the fiction writer and when the two overlap, problems can arise. Sandra Worth's emotional desire to address the truth of the past, which is not atypical of writers who cover particularly emotive subjects (in her case, the life of Richard III), prevents her from questioning her own assumption of that truth, for instance. Likewise, the writer's conception of the past can be appropriative. Writers of fiction have cultural and ethical responsibilities towards the history they use in their fiction.

Historical ethics assumes an ideal situation of cultural neutrality; that is, that history should be non-appropriative. This is a vexed issue for historians and cannot be explored here. However, a fiction writer's narrative can also unintentionally draw on the writers' own privilege (provided by their personal background, such as their class, their ethnicity or their gender) and use it to shape a history that meets the assumptions of this background. The assessment of Richard III by someone from another kind of background might be very different. From the perspective of someone outside the English-speaking world he might be seen as a minor king of no great importance, for his international dealings were small and his reign was short. From the perspective of a supporter of the Tudors, he is often seen as a bad king with a proclivity to evil. All of these views are arguable using the work of historians: which one a novelist chooses depends very much on their own background.

This is a problem when the history is appropriative, that is to say when the writer's vision is achieved at the expense of others (usually of others with less power). The various interpretations of Richard III are widespread and so is the argument concerning his fundamental nature: Worth's interpretation of Richard, therefore, is unlikely to be appropriative. An equivalent assessment of Bennelong (c. 1764–813) is more fraught, for there are fewer primary sources and almost all of those are from the perspective of non-Indigenous people. Bennelong's motivations and character are much harder to discover using the historical record and he belongs to a people who are not dominant currently in Australia, therefore any interpretation of him has a higher need of ethical awareness.

The ethical issues imply two fundamental assumptions in relation to writers. The first is that a novelist has an ethical responsibility to their society and to the history they depict and that they should therefore take this into account in the shaping of their fiction. The second is that they do not necessarily have cultural carriage of the subjects they choose to write about. Neither of these questions was discussed by the writers interviewed. Those with emotive responses to history and their subject matter evidently felt that they had cultural carriage of their subjects, however no writer addressed this question directly and only a few addressed it indirectly.

Even if the writers had responded to a direct question on the subject (none was asked) and had discussed their own responses to these issues, there is no simple general answer to the question of who 'owns' a given interpretation of the past and whether it is appropriative for a writer to use it.

It is very difficult to determine before the event if an interpretation of a given event is legitimate or if it undermines an authentic interpretation. An author's background to this determination can be critical, as Helen Darville/Demidenko demonstrated when the author claimed a Ukrainian background rather than her actual English one to give credence to her fictional Holocaust narrative, *The Hand that Signed the Paper* (1995). Furthermore, when a fiction such as *Holy Blood, Holy Grail* (where the authors actually planted material in French archives in order to claim solid historical discoveries on their origin-of-Christ story) overrides standard historical interpretation of a subject or place and time in the public eye what does this mean for fiction writers who call upon these works and these ideas?

Ethics and cultural responsibility in its full complexity is beyond the scope of this study, but some aspects can and must be discussed. For instance, one of the questions asked of the interviewees in 2004–5 was: 'What aspects of the past do you feel you can alter for the purposes of a novel?' and 'Why?' In their answers, the writers generally implied consideration of ethical issues relating to transmission of history and interpretation of sources, although not the wider ethical issues just discussed.

Ethics was not, however, a major concern for all of them. Short story writer Michael Barry claims no limits, for example. He will do 'Whatever the traffic will bear – I do what is necessary for narrative needs. If my story is doing too much violence to believability, however, I would shift to another historical period, or convert wholly to "historical-themed" fantasy.' Barry is at the extreme end on this question. More typical is Elizabeth Chadwick, who says, 'I will sometimes hedge around some subjects because either I'm not as interested in them as I should be or I feel that a modern reader might have difficulty.' But also, 'I would never ever alter chronology to suit the machinations of a story. To move a battle or an event is inexcusable. I try to avoid anachronisms of props and window dressing and I try to get inside the cultural mores of the period.' If one summarizes this as 'Take due care,' and if the ethical focus is on the relationship of the novel with known history, then hers is a typical response.

Some writers try for minimal intervention. Sandra Worth can speak for them: 'I honestly try not to alter anything.' She adds, 'Even the emotions my characters feet came from what I believe they must have felt, given their physical and emotional makeup, and their situation at the time.'

This was another subject where there was a clear apparent split between the interviewees writing historical fiction or historical romance and those writing speculative fiction. Those who write speculative fiction tended to belong in the 'Can change most things' group, while those writing historical fiction and romance felt they had a higher level of responsibility towards the history they were using. As Helen Hollick explains, it 'depends on the style of the book, but I believe accuracy should be researched to the author's best ability'.

Maxine McArthur places the whole question in the genre framework, saying it 'depends on your contract with the reader. If you say you're writing an historical novel, I'd say very few [alterations], apart from introducing new characters. If it's an alternate history, the sky's the limit.'

When the question was framed to focus on the historical themes, the same split occurred. The clearer the individual writer's affiliation with speculative fiction, the more they felt they could take liberties with history.

Elizabeth Chadwick put the case for the historical fiction and romance group when she said of those who were not concerned with taking care with the history: 'I say why bother writing a historical story in the first place if that's your attitude?'

When looking more precisely at the question of ethics, however, the reactions of the writers demonstrated that some of them were aware of their ethical relationship with current historical knowledge. Sandra Worth explained this responsibility very carefully:

> I believe that there are degrees of responsibility, depending on what aspect of the market the author is writing for, and depending on that author's readership. Some readers don't require stringent historical accuracy for a satisfying read. Perhaps they just want a 'feel' for the period, and an idea of what went on. Honesty is what counts: don't mislead the reader, and give them what they have come to expect from you.

The ethics are implicit in this and are linked to the reader contract, not with history outside the novel or with the subjects of the novel. The concept of appropriation is not something that is immediately part of the equation. As Catherine Butler explains, it 'depends on the genre being used: there is always a kind of contract between reader and writer. If the latter presents the fiction as historically reliable, then it had better be so.'

One writer, however, considers that the real past behind the historical narrative has implications for the writer's approach to representing history in a novel. Wendy J. Dunn says:

> I try my best to remember my stories are based on real people. I'd never deliberately blacken a person's character for the sake of selling books. But I also recognize fiction writing takes our characters and story in directions we don't expect or plan. Artistic license is a valid part of writing novels – but for historical fiction writers, I think it needs to come out of our research. We should believe it is possible for such an event to have occurred.

Sandra Worth sees the matter as complex, but the responsibility she sees relates far more towards the audience than to the writer's relationship with the sources used. Worth's explanation fits closely with Michael Barry's thought that 'whatever the traffic will bear' is what should be done. For him and for Sandra Worth, the issue is genre dependent. Sally Odgers, likewise, consciously brings in the genre of the particular novel when she assesses this element, saying that the approach to history 'depends on the tone of the book. If it's an erotic novel or bodice ripper or even a romp, then anachronism can add to the fun. If it's a serious novel (even of the pop-fic genre) then I think it very important to stick to fact where possible. I always check the introduction of custom/knowledge/invention/convention as far as I can.'

Catherine Butler describes the relationship between genre and responsibility more precisely, as we have seen. In her discussion of the contract between reader and writer, she moves beyond the simple statement that the fiction should be historically reliable if presented this way and adds, 'As a reader, incidentally, I find the importation of specifically modern attitudes into historical fiction no less grating than the importation of modern technology. Probably more so.' Brian Wainwright, however, adheres closely to his sources and is careful to disclose his relationship with them when he knowingly modifies what he receives from them:

> I think it very important, and that conscious diversions should be noted and declared to the reader in an afterword or similar. For example, I felt guilty about having Sir Thomas Erpingham fighting at Shrewsbury (1403) when he was actually in Ireland. However, I found this out at a late stage and it would have meant a substantial rewrite and yet another character to replace him. So, in the end, I left him there and declared the distortion.

Chadwick expresses this view clearly when she says, 'Personally I consider it very important, but I know there are others who feel it's not so much of an issue.'

There is no conflict between these views. Dave Luckett, in fact, explains the apparent contradiction, when he says about the responsibility of the writer:

> I wouldn't have thought that it was of any importance whatsoever, if it were not for the fact that narrative built on the idea of cause and effect imposes its own constraints. If, for example, you use horses for transportation, that means that your cities cannot grow beyond a certain size. But there are more subtle effects. For example, overland trade of bulk commodities is impossible. Not difficult: impossible. So large-scale steel production, which relies on bringing together serious tonnages of coal and iron ore, is

also impossible unless both of them occur on navigable rivers, which is very unlikely. That, in turn, means steel will be expensive and prized – and it'll be made in small pieces only, but it also means that an ideally situated city might be able to specialise. It means that cities can only grow on navigable waterways, and if your ship technology is, say, fourteenth-century, this would include only relatively enclosed seaways. If your economy is entirely agrarian, with no large scale industry, then the control of land becomes the overwhelming preoccupation of the ruling elites, and that gives rise to a whole series of social institutions and customs, which must be consistent with it.

This explanation, although lengthy, is clear about what the author's responsibility is and why different writers take apparently different views to the underlying ethical questions relating to the use of history in fiction.

It all relates to the role that history plays in a given narrative, and this relates very closely to the setting. History is a part of the world that is built for the novel, and where that world fails, the novel is more precarious. As Helen Hollick says, 'the novel should at least be plausible regarding accuracy. *No* historical fiction book can, by its very nature, be totally accurate.' There is no clear single boundary of responsibility: it shifts according to the genre needs and audience needs of the novel, and according to the writer's own perception of their narrative's relationship with history.

4. Transparency

How far should a writer go to explain their reasoning and research to their readers? How much of their research should be transparent and able to be verified?

An author's note on a website or at the back of a novel is not the same in kind or in level of detail and explanation as the critical apparatus that historians use to achieve transparency. It is almost impossible for a work of fiction to achieve the kind of intellectual transparency that is essential for scholars, because the inclusion of detailed footnotes or endnotes and a critical bibliography would render the work of fiction significantly less marketable.

Not even the literary writers using intellectual approaches to history as key themes (for instance, authors such as Umberto Eco, John Fowles, and Hilary Mantel) break the reader contract so far as to disrupt the narrative with a full critical apparatus. This means that the best a writer can do in relation to transparency is take due care in the research and explain (in an author note, in interviews, in afterwords of various lengths) that due care has been taken.

In order to take due care, the author needs a means of evaluating their sources, both the experts they consult and the primary sources. The transparency of the scholarly historian may not be achievable, but the thinking that lies behind the research process is critical to the success of the work. Not all primary sources are reliable in the same way. Not all histories tell the same tale. The example of William I is useful here, for there is a clear divide into versions of his history: the English (where William may be depicted in a negative light and described as having killed the last of the English kings and harrowed the North of England) and the French (where William is considered a good lord, bastard son of a great leader). How do authors assess primary and secondary sources?

Dave Luckett says he evaluates potential sources 'by their caution':

> If they don't know, they say so. They specify where the assertion comes from. They quote sources, in standard form. They state the original evidence, and then clearly tell you where they are extrapolating or inferring. They don't ask questions like 'Had we really found Camelot?', because I'm always tempted to reply, 'Possibly, but more likely it's somebody's horse-trough. Or maybe their privy.'

Brian Wainwright adds experience into the mix:

> Experience plays a part. I read a lot of reviews, because if an academic work has flaws, the author's peers are usually quick to spot them and are better qualified to do so than I am. I try to read all sources critically; this applies even to primary sources. I have learned that medieval chroniclers were biased and that medieval clerks often made sloppy mistakes.

Approaching sources, either living or dead, is an ongoing process and develops as an understanding of a subject and its sources develop. Even without the need to explain the process as part of the final product, authors need to validate information. Sally Odgers explains, 'I cross check information, and sometimes look at the writers' track records', while Robyn Starkey turned it into a teaching moment: 'I wrote an interactive module to show my students how to do this. I look at who wrote it, who recommended it, who published it, stuff like that.'

This set of processes closely resembles what many undergraduate history students learn: the weighting and evaluation of sources (both primary and secondary), the development of context and understanding and the skills to continue learning. The process of seriously researching for a planned work of fiction provides an apprenticeship in some of the basic skills that historians possess. The level of these skills is patchy, with some writers developing them at a more sophisticated level than others. If writing history into fiction is a history apprenticeship, it is one with no standardization. Nevertheless, those basic historical research skills are part of the writer's toolbox and are essential for careful world building.

The four elements of research, interpretation, responsibility and transparency are just as critical to novelists therefore, as to historians, but operate somewhat differently. The world the historian builds is as accurate a representation of the past as the researcher is capable of, within the confines of knowledge, understanding and historical narrative. The fiction writer works from a world that they have created for the novel itself.

***

Between the research and the novel rests the vast flowing river that is extrapolation. Extrapolation is a process by which the writer of fiction transforms history into narrative. It precedes interpretation, that is, the material extrapolated is interpreted, thus creating the world of the novel. In creating this background to their tale, the writer relies on some primary assumptions on the relationship between history and fiction. How mutable is history when being transformed into fiction? This is the question that remains once the four categories are accounted for: what is the difference between a historical narrative and a fictional one? This is related to how writers actually develop the world of the story. It is not simply a matter of researching history: it is a matter of transforming it into narrative. One of the issues that need to be examined to understand how that transformation occurs is how writers work to determine whether there is a transition from one zone (a research zone) into another (story space for writers; that is, a writing zone). How do writers master their sources and extrapolate research into story?

Margo Lanagan (Polack, *Europa*, 2014) enters the space of her story with a high level of awareness that this is what she is doing:

> I have to have a bit of time (for a short story this might only be a matter of a coffee break!) between the researching and the sitting down to write the story. Ideally I do the reading and the exploring and the scrapbooking, pack it away into my subconscious, walk away from it la-la-la pretending not to look at it.
>
> Then when I sit down to write the story the elements I started with, around which I did your research – usually the narrating character and the gist of the climactic scene – will have become infused with the relevant parts of what I've found out about their world, and the details of the research will pour out all of a piece with the story and character.

For some writers, the first step is preparative. Kathleen Cunningham Guler says:

> I master my material by reading, asking questions, then reading some more, until I get a clear visualization of the setting, the characters, and as many details as I can find. When I have the blessing of being able to travel to historical sites, I am able to confirm or correct what I have studied. Visiting the sites will also open more questions to be studied on returning home. Once this visualization occurs and I can see it clearly in my mind, I will sit down and start writing. Admittedly, I will watch some movies to help capture the mood of the piece I'm working on, but movies are more for inspiration, not mastering material.

Elizabeth Chadwick's process focuses on the needs of the novel above all, that is to say she deals with source material and masters it as part of a carefully planned approach to writing. This was discussed in Chapter 4, as was Catherine Butler's combination of careful research and 'letting it compost.' Sophie Masson also puts the needs of the novel first, always, with her search for the texture of the novel and the need to weave a story shape.

Brian Wainwright's response suggests that he may not be clear within himself about specific aspects of how he extrapolates: he knows what he does and how important it is to him, but he searches for ways of explaining it. His suggestion as to how he masters his sources is the following:

> Dare I say imagination, based on years of reading and other research? Sometimes I have to think about where people used to go to exchange secrets – one reason why many of my scenes take place either in bed or in a garden!

> I don't really understand the process myself. I visualise the scene, and off I go. It often develops as I write it and new ideas pop up. Rarely, I pinch pieces of chronicle-recorded dialogue and fit them in. (For example there are a couple of genuine Richard II quotes and a whole recorded conversation of Henry IV in *Fetterlock*.)

Wendy Dunn's answer suggests that matters may not be cut and dried. For her, it is not about the material, it is more about the actual moment of writing:

> Best of times for me as writer is when it feels I've stepped into a plane of existence and I'm hardly aware I'm typing – just in another time and place. But if I make choices now how to play it, I try best to let my characters talk about the important things to them and their stories. Especially if it can help to show their growth.

Kari Sperring (an English writer who, as Kari Maund, is also a practising historian) considers world building and writing part of a single process, of which extrapolation is a key aspect. In an email dated 17 July 2015, she explains:

> I am often learning about the world in which I'm working as I go along. So, with *Living with Ghosts*, I knew there was a city and I knew it had a river and many bridges, and was in some ways a bit like seventeenth century Paris, but that was it, really. I found out what it looked and sounded and smelled and felt like as I and the characters went along.

Her description of the process is that 'Often it's small things that are key for me – the light in *Grass King* (that sepia quality you get in the late evening is summer in Spain, say); the ways different areas of cities smell different to each other.' She operates instinctively for the most part, by feel. 'Places and social structures follow feel,' Sperring explains, 'I don't know, for instance, why women occupy all the places of power in *Living With Ghosts*, it's just how the book needed to be.' This sense of the organic is important. It suggests that story space for some writers begins much earlier than when research is finished. In fact, it suggests that for at least some authors, that story space and research have a troubled relationship.

US fantasy writer Marie Brennan (email correspondence, June 2015) also describes an extrapolative process that has an organic feel, although the term she uses is 'spiral'. She explains that her story ideas 'often begin with something about the setting (that anthropology background action) and characters in an interesting relationship to that aspect of the setting.'

> *With Fate Conspire* began with me thinking 'if in the Elizabethan period there was a faerie court hidden underneath London, as I wrote about in *Midnight Never Come*, then what would happen to them when the Underground starts punching iron rails through their home?' That gave me concrete dates, so I went and started learning about what else was going on in London around that time. Originally the book was going to start in 1870; in fact, I think I even began writing it with that date in mind. But then I came across references to the Fenian bombings on the Underground in the 1880s, and since I'd already decided that one of my protagonists was Irish, I reset the story to 1884. So the research and worldbuilding gave me starting points to develop my story, and then the story itself calls for additional world.

Laura Anne Gilman sees her process somewhat differently to Lanagan and Sperring (email correspondence, June 2015); she explains:

> For the most part, the idea for a world comes to me in a flash – a turn of a phrase or a question that settles into my brain and spins out the 'What if?' moment into something more solid – a sense of time and place and politics. Then the story and the world spin out together, each building on each other – if a character does a thing, if a plot line turns thus, what sort of world causes/creates that reaction? And then what I build from that further informs the character/plot, rinse and repeat until we get to the end of the book ...

This suggests, however, that the history in the novel is not linked to the way the novel is conceived for all novelists: for some it is an aside, for others (the historical fiction writers we have already discussed) it is critical, and for others still, it is entirely irrelevant. As we saw earlier, genre matters.

Marie Brennan describes the place she writes her novel from as a 'thought map' and suggests that a narrative space built for many stories might be researched and built quite differently from that built for a single novel. She explains:

> The *Dragon Age* series of games are a great example of how to build narrative space for a franchise, because the designers clearly went through and asked themselves 'What different groups are there in the world? What conflicts do they have? What history together?' So instead of the world being built for a single story (darkspawn invading; you have to defeat the Archdemon that leads them), it's built for a lot of stories: dwarven caste conflicts, elves as an oppressed underclass on the verge of revolt, mages vs. the Templars who are supposed to watch over them, heresies within the Chantry, etc.

Extrapolation is part of a wider process the writer undertakes. In the field of science fiction and fantasy, this is often referred to as 'world building'. At this point, it helps to bring world building into the shaping of the novel, for it gives essential context for the processes. The scope of it and the history it draws upon can vary according to the scope of the novel as well as according to the writer's concept of sufficient and appropriate world building. A writer will reach out and research history more carefully and with far more focus if they are writing a novel which has history as a key focus. The way a writer shapes their novel, in other words, predicts the genre, which then controls their probable approaches to research.

As we have seen, world building is, literally, building the world of the novel. It can entail creating a map and setting locations. It can involve research into the history that the writer will incorporate into the novel, or the development of the background of various characters. It can include everything from land formations to political structures and social mores. Historical fiction writers have referred more to researching our world, our history, that is to say, formulating a world for the novel from material that is already known to historians than to building a world. They are not creating a world, in their eyes, but understanding the one that already existed in our past. In general, when writers referred to using history in their fiction, they implied using a known world (history) as the basis for their fiction.

When a fiction writer uses history to build the world of the novel, therefore, they are negotiating between quite different places. They read/ experience the work of the historian in order to create the world for their novel. How they move from one to the other depends very much on the writer. Marie Brennan implies, for example that, in her work, she does not simply move from researching and building the world into writing. Once she is writing, she can very easily drop back into historical research. She has to pause the writing 'when the story heads for a blank bit of the map':

> If I haven't really thought about the government of the country the story is taking place in, but suddenly my characters need to go to court, then I have to stop and figure out what court is going to look like.

Writers work uniquely in the movement between research and the finished novel. Even if they are in accord in how they consider history or the sorts of historical illustrations they use, their processes using them are intuitive and individual.

The flexibility described by these writers means that, even when writers rely on the four factors that historians use, they use the material derived from the research and interpretative stages in distinctive ways. How they adapt their historical material to meet the needs of the novel illuminates why research, interpretation, responsibility and transparency can be interpreted differently for different styles of writing.

Michael Barry and Chaz Brenchley are a useful starting point for exploring this, for their views are close. Barry explains in relation to changing material to meet his writing needs that he will do, 'Whatever the traffic will bear – I do what is necessary for narrative needs. If my story is doing too much violence to believability, however, I would shift to another historical period, or convert wholly to 'historical-themed' fantasy.'

This is quite different to the position of Elizabeth Chadwick, who explains, consistently with her other comments, that:

> I will sometimes hedge around some subjects because either I'm not as interested in them as I should be or I feel that a modern reader might have difficulty. For example, I'm not a religious person myself and while I find spirituality interesting, I find church politics and who's bishop of this or archdeacon of that incredibly tedious. Talk about the Medieval Church and I turn into Sleeping Beauty in the *Shrek 2* film when she falls snoring out of her coach. So I tend not to do that much religion in my novels. However I'm aware that it was a bigger deal for my medieval characters.

Sandra Worth works from within the story. She says, 'I honestly try not to alter anything. Even the emotions my characters feet came from what I believe they must have felt, given their physical and emotional makeup, and their situation at the time.'

Even Dave Luckett, with his higher level of awareness of the mutability of history to fit the needs of a fantasy narrative, explains that:

> Events and personalities can be altered at will, but the setting must still be self-consistent. Any recognisably medieval setting must include the basic economic facts about the society and the practices and institutions that arise from them. For example, I recently read and strongly criticised a novel set in a medieval society where a prince eloped and had the resulting marriage recognised, and where one of the institutions was for the king to appoint viceroys to rule in his name over large areas of his own kingdom. Both of these are impossible, of course.

Robyn Starkey clarifies that these differences are due largely to genre:

> I think it would depend on the book. If I were writing historical fiction, I wouldn't want to deliberately alter things. I hate when people write medieval fiction and the characters have twentieth century worldviews. Maybe that's why I don't write historical fiction.
>
> On the other hand, writing fantasy, I think it is cool to play around with this stuff all the time.

Why is genre so important to the mutability of the history in the novel? Catherine Butler spells it out, indicating that it is a readership issue. She explains that she does not deliberately fabricate the past:

> ... except in the trivial sense that this is fiction and therefore not a description of what really happened. As a general question, I'd feel happy altering anything if there was a good reason for it, but I would have to take into account the experience of the noticing and well-informed reader, whom I would prefer not to irritate with pointless inaccuracies.

This suggests that the writers see that audiences are differently informed and that they assume that the readers of historical fiction expect higher levels of historical precision (that is, higher levels of correspondence between the

historical narratives of historians and those of the novelist) than speculative fiction writers.

Felicity Pulman demonstrates how this audience interface affects the
writing. It all comes down to credibility, which demonstrates again how
importance the credibility of the history within the fiction is to the relationship of fiction with history. 'You tread a fine line here!' she explains.

> If your fictional characters interact with real characters and events in your fiction,
> obviously you have to invent situations in which this might happen. To retain cred-
> ibility you couldn't just cancel (for example) the Plague or the French Revolution,
> but I think it's okay to alter small aspects of historical events so long as they don't
> alter the sense (and outcome) of the real events.

One of the key factors in credibility from this particular angle is how
modern characters feel to the writer and readers. Sophie Masson says:

> I think you can do all sorts of things – can fill in 'gaps' – for example, not much is
> known of Marie de France's life, so I could imagine it, based on her work and the
> personality that emerges through it. I think you can also do 'alternate' visions of his-
> tory. What I don't like is when people try to make historical characters too modern;
> that's like Anglicising foreign characters, it's silly and artificial.

Artist and audience share these approaches to characters, for the vast majority of writers are also readers, with opinions as readers. Writers are trans-
lators for other readers, in fact, as Wendy Dunn suggests when she talks
about 'The unknowable past. What happens behind closed doors. The
emotional journey and growth of historical personages. If there is no way
of no knowing, it frees us to be creators by using the framework of history.' Speculative fiction writers (ranging from Chaz Brenchley to Michael
Barry) at their most extreme consider that the material they draw upon for
their fiction is almost frighteningly mutable and even the more conservative speculative fiction writers believe that their material is at the service
of the novel, primarily, and that they do not have a wider duty towards
history. Historical fiction writers, however, have a tighter respect for their
sources and do not feel that they can change things at will: the story has
to come first, but it also has to conform to a much higher degree to their
source material.

This opens the question of what fiction writers offer that comes less easily to historians. One answer to this is point-of-view. Historians usually have a static narrator (themselves) who operates in the limited realm of what can be known and how the sources can be used to inform or expand or interpret this. Narrators in fiction are, as Kay implies, far more flexible. They can indicate the unreliability of our understanding of the past, or suggest special insights. They can offer alternate points of view. This clarifies the relationship between the interest in the Middle Ages expressed by, for instance, Debra Kemp and her passion to tell one particular story: for her, Arthurian history is not something that belongs to a dry, third person narrator. She sees it as flowing from and around the character. Fictional narrative can be fluid.

This potential fluidity is the factor that explains the difference between the historian and the fiction writer when discussing research, interpretation, responsibility and transparency. The fluidity works to enhance credibility and relates to the form (and therefore to the genre) of the novel.

CHAPTER 7

How research affects the novel

World building is not a simple matter. One reason that writers' processes are complex and fluid is because the material they translate into narrative is complex. Moreover, any work of fiction claiming precision in its history has to work through a series of issues, from the nature of its sources through to what kind of assumptions it makes concerning the nature or specifics of a historical period. Authors must contend with modern views of particular periods, which sometimes have led to a wholly inaccurate depiction, as is often the case with contemporary fictional depictions of the Middle Ages. A classic example of this is T. H. White's *The Once and Future King*, whose interpretation of the early Middle Ages, although clearly using whimsy and allegory and fantasy rather than Early Medieval history, has deeply influenced modern narratives concerning that period.

In a way, history plays the same role as a character or set of characters in a novel, and research is essential when that character is central and less essential the more peripheral the history becomes. In the case of Peter Dickinson's Merlin in *The Weathermonger* (1968), the role of the historical/literary Merlin was so unimportant that serious research would have actually undermined the novel. Dickinson explains: 'I didn't do any research at all. I relied vaguely on my memory of Arthurian stories' and 'I wanted Merlin rather vague, but marked by symbols of power' (Thompson, 1999). The reason the research was cursory and almost non-existent therefore was because Merlin was not being used for his historical or literary value; Merlin was, to use Dickinson's words, 'a piece of mechanism'. At the other end of the spectrum, Guy Gavriel Kay is a fantasy writer who undertakes considerable research. In an interview (Auden 2010) he indicates a pattern of about a year's research for a given novel. The nature of the research and whether or not it links to the work of historians depends very much therefore on the nature of the novel and the purpose to which history is put in that novel.

From another angle, we can see how the nature of the historical record affects the way research influences novels. Many of the similarities between Hilary Mantel's *Wolf Hall* and Philippa Gregory's *The Other Boleyn Girl* are due to overlap in the type of sources they use. In earlier periods, most of the surviving sources are formal, for instance the records of the adhesion debate for France in the early fourteenth century are far more common than private letters from the same place and time. This means we have relatively little information concerning personal lives in fourteenth-century France compared with sixteenth-century England, for which there exists a far greater array of sources including a significant number of private letters and household documents. Mantel and Gregory are able to establish a more detailed understanding of their chosen place and time than if they had set their novels in fourteenth-century France. The increased number of sources available for European history as we approach the present and as literacy became a more normative part of culture enables this.

However, the sources themselves still shape that historical understanding through the nature of what was written down, what survives and what is accessible and what has been interpreted by historians. Philippa Gregory and Hilary Mantel share some characteristics largely because they do not use clinical data about Tudor England: they rely on written sources that have strong characteristics in style and the types of information they carry. These written sources, whether they be letters, literary texts or court proceedings, are major factors in shaping the writer's understanding. Overlaps in source material can lead to a similarity of approach to the subject.

Overlap in approaches by novelists may also come from a reliance on published or translated sources, for example Elizabeth Chadwick and Sharon Kay Penman both use the English Pipe Rolls. Primary sources shape writers' responses to history just as much as secondary, thus the nature of the historical record (what is published, what is available, what is translated) is critical.

Many writers are aware of this and try to query historical sources from new angles. However, they may not find what they need if they seek help from a historian or from historical studies on a subject related to their fiction to flesh out their understanding of their chosen period. When interviewed, Brian Wainwright expresses frustration that asking an expert does not often lead to the type of answers that he needs at a given point for his fiction. Many of the writers interviewed have developed techniques for handling these problems. Elizabeth Chadwick explains:

> These days I have a reasonable working knowledge that tends to sort the good stuff from the bullshit at the outset. With books I tend to plump for academic publications i.e. the university presses, Boydell & Brewer, Sutton et al. and for recognized academic authors – David Crouch, Robert Bartlett, Matthew Bennet, etc. Also I buy translations of primary sources. With web pages I will use those recommended on academic e-lists and I will always look for footnotes and sources.

This is equivalent to a historian's assessment of the reliability of sources, despite its different end use. Chadwick is taking care with her sources and consciously shaping her understanding of them.

Sandra Worth applies this care to the work of professional historians when she says:

> If they are a recognized authority, I tend to put more credence into what they are telling me, such as a PhD at a known university. Even then, I use my own judgement, and I try to corroborate whatever I decide to use with one other source. There have been too many cases where an authority made a statement that later proved erroneous. I use web pages just for interest, but I don't use anything from them unless it can be corroborated elsewhere, usually a university source (academic paper, book, article).

We have seen in the previous chapter that Dave Luckett assesses experts 'By their caution. If they don't know, they say so.' Catherine Butler is in a similar intellectual position and operates 'sceptically':

> I generally use the Net to get an angle on where to find reliable information, rather than stopping there. I try to consult several books on any one subject so as to get a 'feel' for the range of opinions and approaches.

Kathleen Cunningham Guler, likewise, advances with care:

> I have learned, after studying Arthurian Britain and Celtic history for more than twenty years, that any book or other source (especially the internet) should be

approached with caution. Just because it is published doesn't mean it is accurate. To have access to a scholarly email list to see the consensus of opinion on a particular work has been a blessing. I can be more meticulous than a journalist – I'll go through several sources on a single detail before I feel comfortable that it can be used. I learned this the hard way with my first book, which had a couple of blundered details in it that could have been easily checked. Most readers (unfortunately) would never know the difference, just like movie-goers, but there will always be one out there that has to rake the author over the coals for a mistake, no matter how minor.

Nicole R. Murphy, on the other hand, uses her 'feel' for the material:

> If it's a well-presented argument and there is evidence to back them up, then I will listen to them. I think if they are rambling or covering too many topics at once, then you need to consider whether they know any subject in depth enough. Anyone that writes a book about one particular topic, filled with evidence to back what they say, will be someone I will pay attention to.

The level of control the writer exercises over their sources (whether primary, secondary, or a verbal consultation with a subject expert) thus depends very much on the writer's awareness of the need to use care. They all operate with a certain level of awareness and criticism, whatever level of sources they are examining. Some, however, like Chadwick, develop their own body of knowledge to use as a counterpoint, that is to say, they will not accept the assumptions and views presented by their sources. They will query more specifically and add the information and understanding gained to the historical world they have already built for their fiction. Others will accept their source material as presented and use it as the main building block for the world of their novel.

The particular problem the fiction writer faces is that where any given subject area is not directly addressed either by themselves or by their sources, a popular assumption probably exists to take its place. Furthermore, as Brian Wainwright said when interviewed, 'one cannot assume all readers have a PhD in Medieval History': the final work has to tell a story that is comprehensible without critical apparatus and explanations of abstruse subjects. These matters have already been addressed.

Where an author stands in terms of world building, understanding of sources, level of investigation and interpretation depends on various factors. Writers can draw on self-discipline and rigorous application of intellect (Chadwick and Guler are good examples of this, as discussed earlier). They can draw on passion for the subject, pushing and demanding greater depth (Dunn and Worth) and making more extensive inquiries until their emotional needs are met. They can draw on professional discipline by examining their technical requirements and rigorously meeting them.

Some novelists fall into the same category as Dickinson and his Merlin and do not research much. Michael Barry defines the history he needs according to what is readily attainable and usable. This is often genre-related. Writers who define themselves as writing fantasy define themselves as having a smaller burden of historical research, by and large, than those who define themselves as writing historical fiction or historical romance. It is important to note that this smaller burden does not in any way reflect the writer's academic background, their strength in intellectual disciplines, or their level of interest in history. Authors who take on a higher burden of research may entirely lack university qualifications: Elizabeth Chadwick is an excellent example of this. The amount and nature of research is more linked to the style of novel than to any other single criterion.

The mixed responses writers give to all the research questions in the interviews suggest that writers may not have a fixed or even shared view of what historical research is essential for in a novel. This, in its turn, suggests that common themes and approaches to history in genre fiction come from shared culture on a broader level. One approach to establishing if this is the case is to determine the relationship between 'reality' (the publicly acceptable historical narrative) and tales, and also between pageant (the attractive, the spectacular) and the more mundane aspects of history.

Writers were asked about how they break down the history they use in their writing. Their answers help elucidate their processes and the thoughts behind them.

Michael Barry is interested in 'real history', especially when it produced conflicts that might be useful in his narrative. The example he gives is 'John MacArthur's role as father of the sheep industry conflicting with his role as crimelord and Godfather of early Colonial NSW'. In other words, he explains he is 'mainly interested in the grubby stuff'. He is interested in telling story from a particular viewpoint 'for voice especially' and myths and legends are, for him, 'a great insight into the thoughts of people'. This is particularly interesting – for him the myths and legends of a culture bear more of the voice than primary sources such as diaries written by the people who live in that culture. What it means is not necessarily that he does not credit primary sources as giving insights into cultures, but that those insights are not ones he immediately considers for his fiction. It demonstrates, more than anything else, the direction from which many speculative fiction writers approach history. It helps to a certain extent to explain why these same authors feel that history is malleable and changeable.

Dave Luckett, in describing the importance of real people and events to his work, directly addresses the relationship of history with fiction when he points out that these are important 'in the sense that a pig is important to a sausage'. For him, the most important thing of all is the story. The way he explains this underlines the sophistication of his understanding of the relationship between history and fiction. He says that 'this is the most important thing of all, and anyone who doesn't think so shouldn't be writing fiction. Or even narrative history.' If his approach were simpler, the pre-formed narratives of the famous (for narratives grew around them, and are an important part of their fame) would be important to him. Instead, however, he mocks, '"Now let us all praise famous men." No, I think not. It's a fiendishly difficult thing to do. The result is almost always hagiography or demolition, with almost no common ground.'

This response gives some insight into why a writer with formal university training in history would choose the speculative fiction approach, with its lighter burden of accuracy and its frequent distancing from the history of historians. He is dissatisfied with biographical narratives of this particular kind. His statement implies that different kinds of narratives are more interesting and that those different kinds of narratives are not spun from the deeds of famous men.

The sense that the well-known has already been interpreted by the time writers consider them is not at the forefront of Brian Wainwright's thinking on the subject. This difference in articulated awareness explains why this historical fiction writer chooses his particular narrative style and the choices he makes to people his novels.

I prefer to have at least some real people in the mix. This is partly because I tend to write about the 'upper ten thousand' as Trollope called them, and it is faintly ridiculous (to me) to invent new and fictional earls and dukes in a crowded little country like England. Were I writing about townsfolk, for example, I would be much readier to invent characters, although I should still use real people's names if I could. (If the Mayor of Chester was Bill Smith in 1410 it weakens the story, in my mind, to call him Fred Bloggs.) I think to write around them; if you like, they form the trellis around which I interweave my roses.

This is no less sophisticated an approach, but where Luckett's decisions are informed by historiography, Wainwright finds real people important because he is directly linking to standard narratives. He is embellishing and interpreting: in writing his novels, he aligns himself with the modern historical interpretations that ground his research.

None of this is at the expense of story, however. In discussing other aspects of the question, Wainwright adds, as a key qualification, 'it's amazing what stories can be told about mundane lives!' The focus here is on the story.

Wainwright's main focus in his answer demonstrates that he is consciously working alongside known history, and that what is important to him in narrative often comes back to this approach and especially to his choice of central character, here expressed as 'POV' (that is, the point of view character). He writes about

individuals, to a point, but the focus is mainly on 'high society from a different angle'. Oddly, as a male writer, I have tended to use the female POV. In one book this was because I wanted the main character to go to some places where a man could not go, and in the other the book was essentially the story of a particular woman so her POV naturally was centre stage. In some ways it is more interesting to write from an angle where the protagonist, even if well born, does not have easy access to levers of power, but has to use indirect means and faces sundry social and cultural handicaps. I also happen to enjoy writing about women.

Even when discussing how important myths and legends are to him, he returns to the history. 'Much of history is just that – myths and legends; propaganda was not invented by Dr Goebbels, nor yet by King Henry VII,' he explains. 'However, if we are talking Arthurian myths, for example, my writing era is not "far back" enough for them have more than a literary significance. I actually prefer to ground my writing on more prosaic issues.'

Contrast this with Felicity Pulman's approach, where the core theme she returns to is not Luckett's historiography combined with the importance of story, nor Wainwright's relationship with narrative history. Pulman writes both historical fiction (the Janna Mysteries, where Janna solves mysteries in an England racked by Civil War) and speculative fiction with historical underpinning. Her timeslip novels, *Ghost Boy* and *A Ring through Time*, are based on historical research and have a contemporary teenager pulled back in time or meeting an element of the past. *Ghost Boy* (2004) is set on the Quarantine Station in nineteenth-century Sydney, and *A Ring Through Time* (2013) is a convict story, set on Norfolk Island. *I, Morgana* (2014) is the story of Morgana, Arthur's sister, based on popular Arthurian tales and set in an alternate Earth, linked to ours through a portal.

Given that Pulman's writing is not all in the same sub-genre, her response to the question of what is important may give us additional insights into this complex relationship of writers with history. Real people and events, for instance, are important, she says, 'only if they have relevance to my plot'. Decisions regarding point of view and even myths and legends are all mediated by the needs of that particular story.

As we have seen elsewhere, Pulman takes on the research mantle and interpretative approach to history of the historical fiction writer for the most part, but underlying this is the pragmatic approach of the speculative fiction writing. 'Myths and legends were central to my Shalott trilogy. There may be a fleeting reference to the legend of King Arthur in The Janna Mysteries, but that's all.' Story is paramount and the needs of story inform subordinate choices.

Kathleen Cunningham Guler sums up this hierarchy, which is expressed differently by different writers, but which is common to them all:

> All of these are important, but the most is writing a good story. Without a good plot and characters, no one will read the book. The reader must become a part of the characters' lives or else the author will have failed in the storytelling quest.

Like the other writers questioned, she qualifies this, noting that

> telling a story from an unexpected viewpoint and/or from the point of view of individuals or groups forgotten by history has been important as well. Rather than

merely retelling the same story over again, new perspectives told through a different set of eyes can breathe new life into an old tale.

> If a real event and real people can be identified, then they belong in the story. If these cannot be proven as real, as is the case with the Arthurian matter, then I use the legend in as logical a way as possible to attempt to make a realistic historical setting.

Thus it is not a simple hierarchy ranging from the less-researched to the more-researched narrative. Story informs all important elements and enables the writer to make suitable narrative choices. This is fundamental to fiction writers, however they express it. The story aspect is the narrative itself and by choosing to write a novel, they have implicitly created a hierarchy with story as the senior and controlling point. How story works and how history works within story varies considerably from writer to writer, but they share a narrative heart.

The different choices made by writers on how to turn their material into story and even what material is selected and which narratives are chosen contain a range of decisions. While many of these are non-contentious (describing London as being a city in England is seldom contentious), others are not as innocuous. While the relation of writers with history is discussed throughout this study, one aspect of historical interpretation or reinterpretation through story needs special focus. It has already been discussed briefly in Chapter 6 in the context of the writer's responsibilities.

All history that is included in fiction that does not come from the writer's own background is alien that is, it is not within the writer's personal experience, to a lesser or greater degree. At its best the material that comes from outside the writer's background is benign historical cultural adaptation or borrowing. When there are negative impacts from the use or re-use of some else's heritage or when the writer's interpretation changes the public interpretations in ways that have negative impact on specific groups or that change their own use of their culture without their consent, this can be considered cultural appropriation. This has been explored for speculative fiction in Polack (2015).

As we have already seen, the interviewed writers were not questioned about ethical issues in this regard. In a public debate about historical fiction and its public in the *Southern Literary Journal* other writers present a clear indication that ethical considerations and particularly issues of appropriation and reinterpretation ought to be central considerations within the framework a writer uses to tell stories.

As Ellison (1969: 74) explained when describing the issue of interpreting history when there was no public agreed narrative, or when using stories to which one might not be 'entitled' (the contention at this point was US Black history), 'The moment you put yourself in a book, the moment you put any known figures into the book, then somebody is going to say, "But he didn't have that mole on that side of his face …" Facts are a tyranny for the novelist. Facts get you into all of this trouble.'

Academic discourse permits more historical nuancing and more corrective action due to its narrative style. Footnotes and endnotes, non-linear narratives, critical apparatus in general: these permit reservations to be expressed and doubts to be raised without jeopardizing the overall narrative. This is a critical element of the dynamic in scholarly history alluded to earlier.

Popular fiction cannot take the path of enacting a complex critical dynamic without losing many of its readers. Story is the most important element in the novel, not creating a discourse on a subject that will lead to deep understanding. This reinforces the writer's need for more linearity in the narrative and reduces the writer's capacity to use critical apparatus to bring nuance to the discussion. Many novels achieve illumination and understanding on a subject, but this illumination and understanding is seldom achieved in an environment where that critical dynamic can operate. Journals such as *Rethinking History* are pushing at this restriction through changing the formal historiographic discussion, but it is unlikely that these changes will affect anything but a small sector of the reading and fiction writing public. When Umberto Eco uses critical theory in his novels, for example, only a few readers extract it.

This leads to the inevitable statement: fiction is not culturally neutral. History, likewise, is not culturally neutral. The constraints of the novel form themselves help to shape subjects for readers and that reshaping has ethical consequences. Story is king in the world of the novelist who uses history, but this is not a statement without ramifications.

The novel rests upon research foundations. Even if a novel only uses the smell of an oily rag as its fuel for historical interpretation, most authors undertake research in order to find that oily rag. The past is based on modern historical narratives; that is, that the reader has a sense of history from the novel that matches the one they get from their general knowledge or that the challenge of interpreting the history in the fiction. The detective tale set by having William of Baskerville as a main character in a medieval mystery novel, for instance, gives a strong clue that the history is to be unravelled and mistrusted just as much as the characters in Umberto Eco's *The Name of the Rose*. Even if the past depicted within the story is impossible, it needs to be credible.

Despite the general tendency of writers to extrapolate from research following their genre needs, there is not a clear equation of sub-genre with research style, approach and method. The genre link is important, in other words, but it is not inevitable. Deborah Harkness' historical vampire romance *Discovery of Witches* was written by a historian yet only relies on historical method for some aspects of the work, notably those close to the author's own research area. The history and culture of the supernatural protagonists is extrapolated from popular modern understanding, rather than from sources contemporary to the novel's setting or from modern historical approaches to, for instance, studies of vampires or witches in the seventeenth century. This follows the speculative fiction approach to the paranormal, where a magic system is developed for use within the story space, and action happens within those constraints. The framework for all the magical components derives from the built universe and the researched history is more illuminative than integral to this building. Harkness disguises this structure through some clever techniques: the researched history (her scholarly work on alchemical manuscripts) is closely linked to the plotlines and characters and her use of telling detail is very canny, which informs the reader's perception of history in the novel. Thus the reader's perception does not always rely on the level and nature of the historical research undertaken by the writer.

From the historian's view, this is a deplorable departure from the known, especially given that a large percentage of the general public gains their understanding of history from fiction of various kinds. History and fiction are different and have different needs, no matter how much over-lap in their sources and narratives, even when a historian writes a novel.

Most fiction writers also, to be frank, in many cases have different levels of access to sources. Access to sources may be limited by language, skills (how many novelists who set their fiction in the Middle Ages have enough of the technical discipline of diplomatics to interpret document styles accurately, for instance) and archival access. There are areas of history that are understudied (for instance, some regions in the south of France in the later Middle Ages; see the work of Monique Bourin for this), and fiction writers do not necessarily have the time or skills to flesh them out for themselves. Thus, if writers use these settings, they will rely on their imagination and writing skills to flesh out the story.

More than anything, however, time is a luxury for professional fic-tion writers. The amount of historical research required to fill a book of ninety thousand words or more is likely to take years rather than months and few writers receive sufficient income from a single novel to cover years of research. While this book has been researched over a decade, my novel *Langue[dot]doc 1305* only had twelve months allocated to its research. Even then, it was more researched than many novels that use history, for I had been a practising Medievalist for a long time before I began work on this novel. Not only the length of time a writer can give is usually less than optimal from a historian's point of view, but the amount of previous knowledge a writer has of a period and place plays an active part in how effective the research will be. For these reasons, the majority of novelists rely on education, translations, secondary sources and even undergradu-ate textbooks and depend on the accessibility of these sources within a limited time frame.

Historical research requires a wide and varying toolset, but not all novelists possess this toolset and some may not even realize their lack. Underestimating or misunderstanding a place or culture is the most obvi-ous side effect of this. Michael Crichton, for instance, obviously read about polyglottal societies, but demonstrated that he did not understand how they operated (and also that he had not read primary sources in their original languages) by creating an improbable multilingual sentence (1992: 197): 'Anthoubeest, ye schule payen. Quinquesols maintenant aut decem postea.'

These issues add to the divide between the work of research historians and the work of novelists, and they are hard to avoid.

Those few novelists who are also academics, are caught in a bind. As Byatt says (2001: 92): 'It is customary for writer-academics to claim a kind of schizoid personality and state that their research, or philosophical thinking, has nothing to do with their work as makers of fiction.' While the divide is not absolute, for the narratives overlap and even feed into each other, that overlap is complex and it is easier to simplify and say 'Fiction writers represent history in these ways' and 'Academics represent history in these other ways'. While this study breaks down this polarity, it cannot demolish it completely. Jerome de Groot suggests that the work be considered to overlap, rather than be considered the same (2010: 3).

For some writers, research simply is not a key element of the way they perceive their role as creators. If those who prefer a more researched narrative want more freedom in how they can interpret history, they may choose a time and place for which there are few available sources (as Michael Chabon did for Khazaria in *Gentlemen of the Road*) or perhaps a country where few sources exist in a language the author reads (Aliette de Bodard's Aztec trilogy).

All stories are, however, built using limited information. When there is not enough historical or cultural information to create a narrative or flesh out the characters or scenes, the writer will fill in the gaps to create their narrative from within their prior knowledge and understanding of what they need for that particular story set in that particular time. This helps explain why historical fantasy writers often perceive research quite differently to those who write historical fiction.

Initially, however, all novelists are faced with sources. Just like historians, they factor in the date and place of a source, the genre (old letters being differently reliable to old novels, for instance), the audience of the source. The moment the writer begins to think about those sources, they are moving within story space for they are writing from their interpretation of those sources. They have begun to develop the possible world for their particular novel or series when they begin the process of interpretation of those sources to meet their narrative goals.

As we have seen, writers do not necessarily develop formal explanations of this process. When they do not realize that they work within story space from quite early and that their relationship with story space changes during the course of research, they are likely to draw upon their prior assumptions about place and time to create their world; for instance, Connie Willis seldom addresses problems of evidence, furthermore despite having the presence of historians in all her time travel novels, she does not use their voices to address these issues in any depth. Instead, she plays with stereotypes of the period. In some cases (*To say Nothing of the Dog*) this creates an effective past shaped by a world derived strongly from Willis' understanding of Jerome K. Jerome's writing. In others (*Doomsday Book*) the world of the novel draws more upon her own assumptions of a period and place and is thus less plausible. The way those assumptions play out is shown most effectively in *BlackOut (2010)* where Willis uses US coinage in Britain.

The way writers interpret their research can be quite different from the way the historian interprets. Brian Wainwright (in an online conference run by think.com, cited in Polack, 2005) suggests, 'I suppose there's quite a few things we leave out of novels – perhaps, apart from delicacy, because it doesn't advance the story. It's not our job (is it?) to show every aspect of life – we're story tellers, not reconstructionists.' He also points out that the amount of information the writer needs from his sources has very precise limits. 'Period detail is fine,' he explains, 'it helps to set the scene. But is there not a danger it becomes an end in itself? That we end up with a sort of literary re-enactment rather than a story?'

Part of the process therefore consists of value judgements by the writer. How the interviewed writers address the expertise of people they consult, of books, articles and web-pages helps to indicate this. Michael Barry suggests, 'If it is useful to my narrative, the person is an expert and the book is a treasure. If not, they are, respectively, an idiot and a footrest.' Despite Barry's lack of seriousness, overall, writers interviewed are careful and conscientious researchers, who sincerely attempt to establish solid historical foundations for their stories.

So how strong are these writers' sense of responsibility towards accuracy and – more importantly – what else can this tell us?

Dave Luckett was instantly aware of the consequence of the question. The focus is not on the accuracy, so much as on why it is important. The story is the crux. As Luckett explains when he delves into what he means by 'historical accuracy':

> I don't mean the design of a cloak-pin, or what they ate for breakfast. In such a society, what they ate for breakfast was grown or raised within ten miles of where they ate it, and so long as that happens, I couldn't give a toss. Why shouldn't I assume that seed potatoes were brought from America by the Norse in the tenth century, and by the twelfth were in general use throughout Europe? Come to think of it, there's a novel right there.

It is a dynamic relationship. It changes, not just over the long term, but in the moment. It is part of how the writer works within story space and how they develop and draw upon the world they create. The need for accuracy depends upon the needs of the relationship: what does the story require? How can history make the story better? Chadwick and Wainwright consistently come closest to the historian's view of history in other ways, such as their intellectual understanding of the past. This suggests that there is a still a genre link in the attitude towards history.

Helen Hollick, as we have already seen, thinks that fiction cannot, by its nature, be entirely accurate. She thus draws our attention to the fact that the writing of the novel has a complex dynamic. It is not the fact of the past that writers draw upon, it is their interpretation of the world they create and call upon while in their writerly story space.

Once the author has given their manuscript to the editor, there is a set of interventions by both editor and writer to bring the manuscript to publication. This complicates the issue of how accurate the history is in fiction, but it also leaves open the question of when the writer leaves story space and when research for the novel is complete.

The amount an editor intervenes varies considerably. Sometimes the edits are small – preferring one version of a nickname above another – and sometimes they are more considerable. They impact on the nature of history in the final book. A good editor will help polish the work and help realize its potential. Realizing the potential of a work of fiction can have different effects on the underlying approach to history, depending on the nature of the editor.

Publishing houses each have their own approach to these things, which makes it difficult to generalize about the precision of the history in a given novel from the evidence of the final novel alone. In the case of Trivium Publishing, for instance, a list of obvious historical errors is made at an early stage of the reading, and consultation with the author takes place to ensure that very few appear without good reason. This means that the authors are subject to an editing process that includes justification of some of their background research. Other publishers rely on their editors to question historical material that appears problematic. While most publishing houses and editors (most, but not all) will focus on other aspects of the novel (narrative flow, for instance, plot consistency, characterization) rather than this level of precision concerning specific elements of historical detail.

How writers research history for their fiction is complex, therefore, and depends very much on the shape of the world in which the novel is being built, the purposes of the world (what kind of fiction) and the nature of the interfaces between the writer and story space and the writer and their editor.

CHAPTER 8

Genre and presenting the history in the novel

The key factor for the acceptance of the history in the novel for many readers is the way the writer tells the story itself. This rests very heavily on the way the writer thinks a story of that kind should be told. Sandra Worth writes adjectival-rich prose, for example, while Dave Luckett's language is blunter and more concrete. This reflects their conceptualization of history, but it operates within their chosen genre frameworks. Worth's prose is like Philippa Gregory's in vocabulary choices, and, like Gregory, she writes historical fiction with a strong romance component. Luckett's choices reflect his self-definition as a speculative fiction writer, with his descriptions focussed as much on the building of the world of the novel as building relationships within the novel.

Writers make different stylistic choices once they have decided on the direction of their story. To make those stylistic choices a writer begins with genre awareness. Genre awareness, in its turn, rests upon a strong understanding of craft (the tools that create style, plotting, characterization) and genre coding (the signals sent to the reader that help them attribute the book to an appropriate genre and thus to interpret the story).

There is a significant difference between genre awareness and genre coding. Genre awareness is the general sense of where their writing fits that we have just seen demonstrated by Luckett and Worth. It comes from the books a writer reads and by the feeling that 'My book belongs with these and therefore should be classed in the same way.' Worth, for example, has a deep and abiding interest in Richard III and historical novels concerning Richard III. It is unsurprising, therefore, that she not only writes historical novels, but also is aware of what traits a historical novel should possess. This awareness influences the narrative choices the writer makes.

Genre coding can be seen in the technical choices that are made during the writing to push a novel towards a particular genre. These technical choices are critical for communicating the genre to the reader. Awareness of the importance of genre coding (where audience expectations and fulfilment are set up using quite specific narrative conventions) affects what authors choose to write about.

While some forms of modern historical writing are quite close to some forms of fiction by having similarity in aspects of narrative style, the underlying imperatives are still significantly different. Thick description in ethnohistory – where behaviour is described in its cultural and historical contexts – supplies rich detail and is similar in terms of density of information, cumulative effect and non-explanatory nature to some types of information-dumping found in high technology science fiction such as work by Stephen Baxter. An excellent example of how rich the cultural depth of a study such as this can be is in Greg Dening's classic study of the bad language of Captain Bligh (1994), where, by analysing Bligh's behaviour using the surviving written records of Bligh's voyages, he determined that Bligh's poor relationship with his crew was more due to verbal abuse than to any physical ignominy he delivered.

In these cases, the styles and functions of the text have a certain overlap. They inform and they build up understanding through density of information and description rather than by moving a plot forward.

Even when there are apparent similarities between the narratives of the novelist and the historian, they mask fundamental differences: function, form, and purpose of text may look similar on occasion, but they are deeply different. Seitel (2003) suggests that genres are cultural repositories that can then be drawn upon to strengthen how works are read. This agrees closely with the view of genre used here.

The definitions a writer makes of a genre for their own novel are critical to their choices of coding. The novels Luckett and Worth write and the styles they choose reflect the genre, as we have seen, and in turn the coding that is expected of that genre (the military descriptions in Luckett's work) helps ensure that a novel defined by the writer as historical fiction is seen as that by the reader.

This was discussed in earlier chapters, however, pulling it together is important. What is also important is to note that, despite the reinforcement of the genre choice by genre coding in the narrative, if one takes the novels and writers examined overall, the choices fall within a range rather than being an absolute. In other words, within fiction (from the writer's view), there is probably no simple, unified formal definition of each genre.

Patricia C. Wrede (2011) gives one set of definitions, for example, when she explains that Alternate History is fiction 'Where the only thing that's the same as the real world is geography.' She classifies what she calls history-in-fantasy as being 'Secret History' where our knowledge is limited and the novel can reveal the hidden. 'Alternate History With Rivets' extrapolates change from one specific difference from known history; 'Parallel History' is closely related to 'Alternate History With Rivets' but contains significant changes to known history such as in Wrede's own work (which includes the existence of magic while mostly following the general paths of known history). Wrede's definitions are quite different to the definitions the interviewed writers assigned their own work.

Karen Hellekson's study of alternate history novels (2001) takes the same type of novels as Wrede and demonstrates clearly that genre definitions depend on the specific tools used to group works together. While it is also possible to group genres by how action-oriented or character-oriented they are, what prose styles they use, whether they are based on a scientific perception of the universe or on a quite different one, whether they are targeted at an adult or a young adult or a children's audience, whether they are in prose or verse, and so on, these are also groupings made outside the writer's understanding of their own work. The resultant groupings create a sense of what the past is that works within each classification, whether it is all based on Shakespeare's writing (see the Elizabethan fantasy fiction by Sarah Hoyt) or on extrapolating from known history where the beliefs are real: it is, however, an audience-creation rather than an author-creation. The audience perception is too distant from the writer's perception of their own work to be useful in terms of providing insights into how genre affects the writer's telling of history.

***

Examining how writers see some of the terms used throughout this study will provide more insight into how writers explain the history in their fiction and just how different this can be from bird's eye views. Authors were asked to give their own definitions of four terms: fiction, truth, historical accuracy and history.

The term *fiction* was the most interesting, given all writers questioned were writers of fiction. Their definitions help explain how they situate their own novels as narratives.

For Michael Barry, fiction is 'convenient lies' and Sally Odgers explains fiction as 'a story that didn't happen' whereas for Elizabeth Chadwick it is 'a made up story'. These were formal definitions; that is, the writers were looking for something that applied generally rather than a definition that privileged their own work. Sandra Worth obviously had her own work in mind when she defined fiction as 'connecting the dots between known facts': she is one of the writers who sees historical fiction as having an emotive component, as expressing and explaining something important. Dave Luckett links the general question of what fiction is with the narrative world of the fiction writer when he defines it as 'that body of writing that uses imagined narrative to represent some aspect of reality and hence reduce it to comprehensibility'. The key linking component for Luckett is this 'comprehensibility': the interpretative aspect matters.

Brian Wainwright is more precise; he says that fiction is, 'Stories written to entertain, usually including invented speeches and imaginary events. (Rather like *Richard III* by Thomas More.) Historical fiction has the context of an historical background and the author's interpretation of the culture, mores and events of the time.' This aligns with Robyn Starkey's definition of 'Any type of writing which is an exploration of an imagined idea by the author. I think fiction can be researched writing, but it doesn't have to be.' Catherine Butler brings this precision into sharp definition when she says, 'In this context I see "fiction" merely as the description of the literary mode in which I'm working, not as a metaphysical claim.'

There is no single shared definition. The judgments concerning what comprises fiction can be almost clinical, as when Debra Kemp calls it 'an illusion of reality, created for readers to experience, or be passionate about it', or they can demonstrate profound emotion as when Sophie Masson defines it as 'a wonderful story'.

Compare this to the range of responses to the writers' definition of *truth*. Barry links his definition to his definition of fiction by calling it 'inconvenient lies', while Worth connects it to her emotional link with history by defining it as 'the reason I wrote this book'. Elizabeth Chadwick, however, does not take such a simple path. She says that truth is 'hard to define':

> One person's truth is not another's and eyewitnesses differ. I suppose I feel there are two types of truth in historical fiction. What is broadly believed to have happened in the past, and then what more in depth research throws up. Sometimes these are the same, but often they differ. It's the novelist's choice which path to follow ... or indeed go off at a tangent. I think perhaps that integrity matters as much, if not more than 'truth'.

All the other answers fall within the general range of these three. Luckett, for instance, calls truth 'the attempt (never perfectly successful) to represent perceived reality'.

The reason for this particular range is given by Robyn Starkey. She says, 'I really don't care about truth. I don't think it has anything to do with literature, or history, for that matter. Truth is relative.' For some writers, truth is not relevant to their fiction and for others it is almost a binary, that is, truth is the opposite of lie, and their novels are true despite being fictional.

The shading within the definitions given depends on which end of the near-binary of truth/lie writers fall. Butler, for instance, clearly sees truth as relevant, and also as layered. Her definition is an explanation of why this layering is important. She explains, 'I like both the correspondence and coherence theories of truth. The book has to make sense in its own terms, but it also has to *ring* true to the people reading it.'

The need to create a closely personal explanation is something that Wendy Dunn also explains. She says that truth 'is the unmasked essence of humanity – our souls ... it is the difference between pure and unclean. Life is an eternal struggle to keep hold of universal truths shared by all humanity.'

Nicole Murphy explains the relationship between fiction and the outside world, 'There are two types of truth: external and internal truth. External truth means it's true in the real world, internal truth means it's true in the fictional world. I think internal truth is much more important.'

When defining historical accuracy Murphy has far less of a bird's eye view. She thinks in terms of telling detail, rather than in terms of understanding the past through historical narratives. Murphy talks about making sure everything contained in a story is accurate within its particular time period. You can have one type of castle that's accurate, another type of armour that's accurate, but if they did not exist at the same time, it's not historically accurate. It's also important that the way people react to the setting is accurate, so you don't have men just throwing full plate armour onto their bodies, for example.

This is the same approach to period detail and world building that can be seen in the work of many romance writers, and it is interesting to note that Murphy now publishes in that genre as well as in speculative fiction.

Elizabeth Chadwick still works within the confines of the story, but maintains a clear intellectual framework that encases the story and links her narration with her wider sense of history. Historical accuracy for her is

getting it right to the best of my ability. Some things are outside of my scope because I don't have the academic tools to follow them up and frequently not the time to acquire these tools, but within my own limitations I try to recreate an ambience that will make a reader think 'Yes, this is how it might have been.'

Sandra Worth acknowledges the formulation of history and the way it is shaped, but she also wants a precision in the facts she employs that contradicts her acknowledgement. She says, 'History is written by the victors and not all that we have been led to believe is true. That said, historical accuracy is vital to me. If history is worth reading, it must be accurate and no liberties taken with the facts in the story.' Dave Luckett avoids this contradiction when he calls historical accuracy 'the practice of representing the actual economic and social structures of past societies, so far as they are known, or in the absence of knowledge, using logical inference and extrapolation to achieve the same end.' The important difference between these two authors is in genre choice: Luckett avoids the contradiction inherent in Worth's statement in his fiction by writing in genres where that level of precision is secondary. This is particularly interesting given their different choices of expression. Their views reflect their writing at a deep level.

Brian Wainwright avoids the contradiction by accepting the unreliability of what he can know about the past. In the context of a novel, he says that there is a need for verisimilitude in the meshing of the fiction with known history; Anne Neville ought not to appear drinking chocolate or riding a motor cycle. I take the view that where facts are unknown the author may invent, provided the invention is plausible. For example, if a tournament took place on a certain date and we know no more, then I may invent the winner. But if the result *is* known I would not change it to suit the story, nor would I have them playing rugby instead.

His resolution of Worth's contradiction also exposes the main concern of the fiction writer, one which is dealt with elsewhere: historical credibility in the novel can be quite different to historical accuracy.

Felicity Pulman has the best explanation of this relationship. Historical accuracy is, she says, 'tricky. Events that can be verified and cross-checked by various accounts, especially if they're written by eye-witnesses from opposing sides! Always bearing in mind that "history" as such is a comparatively recent concept, and that it is mostly written by the victors who have a vested interest in how the event is portrayed.' Pulman has the same concept of winners/losers as Worth, but has factored bias into her work. At the time of the interviews, Pulman was working on the Janna Mysteries, which required significant amounts of research using medieval chronicles. Her statement is not theoretical, therefore, but directly related to her work at that time. This insight helps explain Worth's apparent contradiction. Her work also uses chronicles, and has been known to take the view of the apparent loser, notably in her first novel, *The Rose of York: Love and War* (2003), which is a strongly Ricardian fictional biography of Richard III.

It is crucially important to keep in mind that these writers are not historiographers or specialists in history theory: their understanding of terms relates, for the most part, to their own work. This work is primarily craft and has quite different social intent to works of scholarly history. These definitions illustrate the extent of these differences. As Wendy Dunn says, 'this is shaped by what shapes us. Historical accuracy depends on our viewpoints and what our tunnel vision allows us to see.'

Moreover, there is a strong link between definition of genre by the author and the level of research the author prefers. While some fantasy writers (Sophie Masson, for instance) carry out significant research, the emphasis is not on the research tying the novel to a real world setting and to a past that actually happened. The emphasis in most of the fantasy writers is in creating a functional or a believable world, that is, one that feels real to the reader. Credibility operates within genre constraints and the writer works within their understanding of genre to make the history in the novel credible. Historical novelists research to recreate the past; fantasy novelists research to create a world.

***

The two poles of fantasy and historical fiction incorporate a fundamentally different idea of what sort of reality they are depicting, how mutable it is, how tied down to the reality of history it needs to be, and how far the writer is *creating* a world as opposed to *depicting* it. However, these two poles (historical and speculative) are not very far apart, despite the differences that have emerged between historical and speculative fiction writers in their approaches and self-definitions. Certain fundamentals apply to most societies, and all writers who use exotic settings need to ground their readers in the reality of those settings. Fantasy writers need to locate water sources for their towns as much as historical romance writers, for instance, and it is (in many cases) far easier to base their worlds on historical research than to invent every small detail, that is to use a town where historical information is available is easier in terms of achieving credibility than creating a functional town from scratch. The principles of the world construction and extrapolation of each of the groups are different, however, even if their sources are the same and even if both groups are using the same period and place for their settings. Essentially, fantasy writers believe that the world can be constructed and built from nothing, giving a feel of the period (and some writers tend more towards this than others) while writers of historical fiction believe that that novel has a firm rooting in a past that really should not be modified.

Self-definition by writers and the nature of the world of the novel (the level at which invention or research dominates) helps explain some of the choices concerning research and extrapolation discussed earlier. As a rule of thumb, the less the writer defines his or her novel as fantasy, the more time they are likely to spend doing historical research for that novel.

The writer's craft is important. How history is used and what precisely is communicated depends very much on the balance of more specific tools the writer chooses at the level of language and close narrative. The choice of balance between use of dialogue, interior monologue, omniscient narrator with present voice or past voice, choice of vocabulary: these can be very potent aspects of narrative and the balance between them has a deep effect on the tale. What the writer does with these and other simple narrative devices helps push the underlying interpretation of the use of history. It helps settle that Donald Barthelme's World War II Arthur in *The King* serves a partly metaphoric role with comic expression to make the medicine go down. The bleakness of the low point of World War II is tempered by the daftness of Arthur being the king rather than George, and the normal dramas of Arthur's story are woven into the fight against Hitler.

Writers using a fantasy Middle Ages, such as Felicity Pulman in her Shalott series, are aided in the establishment of the genre to which their novel belongs by modern Medievalism. Modern Medievalism – that is to say, the popular view of the Middle Ages currently held – includes several possible depictions of the place and time, ranging from political and social (as depicted by Chadwick, for example) to high fantasy. The self-definitions by writers often reflect the type of modern Medievalism they reflect in their novel. As has been discussed (as an aspect of popular assumptions concerning a period) seminal works such as T. H. White's *The Once and Future King* eclipse the reality of the period for many readers, and become a critical part of a writer's own genre definition.

***

Genre definition, as we have seen, is a matter of self-interpretation and also of awareness of where one's work is placed relative to others. Self-definition is supported by tools. One tool that is particularly important in this respect is telling detail. (How telling detail operates in a novel will be discussed in Chapter 9.) The sources of the telling detail in a novel are influences in its use and how the detail is interpreted, for writers are not neutral vectors. What is most important, however, are the interpretations that accompany the use of that detail, whether intentional or not.

Susan Cooper discusses where she obtained her telling detail from for her Dark is Rising sequence (Thompson, 1999). Her links with the past and the emotions that were delivered along with the detail were because she used information coloured by her own memory of a place and time. She checked the topography against ordnance survey maps and she conflated two valleys into one for one section, but much of it came from her own memories. For instance, she explains, 'I can remember going out of the door from my parents' house when I was visiting Aberdyfi from America, to remind myself of what it was like to go across the dunes and down to the sea in the very early morning.'

She reinforced her memory with maps and visits, but her memory was critical. She explains that 'it's not a rational decision. You can't control it. [...] You even find yourself using images from dreams sometimes.' How these techniques are used and how consciously they are used varies from writer to writer: they do not operate as mathematical equations do, producing predictable results upon their careful and clinical application.

History has to belong within the story. Methods for delivering exposition are varied and of varying effectiveness. An expository explanation within a novel can extend the credibility of the narrative through fitting the tone of the novel and using the voice of a character or even a voice given to the narrator.

Samuelson (1993: 198) explains, focussing on writers of speculative fiction, how writers use external consistency and concrete details to communicate the world of the novel so that the reader can interpret it according to their own understanding. This is the primary use of telling detail (or period detail), regardless of the type of novel. The use of telling detail depends very much on the needs of the writer and the specific novel. It can be a window onto a detailed and rich reality, or it can be a static representation that the reader has to fill in for the picture to come to life. Like all other writing techniques, in other words, its use depends very much on the skill and intent of the writer.

George R. R. Martin's use of telling detail, in fact, demonstrates an effective way of using it that can actually *distort* the reader's understanding of the period and place. He inserts the detail to indicate personality rather than to deliver the sense of a precise historical moment. The number of books Tyrion Lannister carries in Martin's *Game of Thrones* series and the ease with which he borrows books from others is key to understanding his character. In terms of cultural values, however, the books are either worth far too little (for medieval manuscripts) or worth far too much (for modern printed texts). Although the cultural value of the books Tyrion encounters and the monetary value is inconsistent, the technique Martin uses to convince us of the books' reality is to keep the emotional value of the books constant within Tyrion's life. Thus Martin distorts the historical status of books, while maintaining their place in his narrative.

The key uses of telling detail are to reinforce the sense of place and time. Through repeating or echoing locational information in William Mayne's *Earthfasts* (1995), very little data is given about the period Nellie Jack Jon emerges from, but we are given over and over the intentionally mystifying information that the lads 'sleep in the wall'. The repetition of the single fact and the eventual explanation that it refers to the specific conditions experienced by the drummer boy in the army at that time highlights the effect of past time entering the present, but it also limits the amount of information Mayne needs to impart concerning that earlier period of time to achieve his effect.

He achieves the use of less actual information concerning that past period by delaying the presentation of any information at all. The suspense and the questions leave not only the modern boys in the dark, but the reader, too. It is the technical opposite of information dumping. In building up the reader's awareness of the importance of the information by building up tension around its delivery, Mayne cleverly builds up the validity of that small piece of the past and ensures that it serves instead of a much more detailed description of place and time.

A sense of the pageantry can affect the same need for less detail. It pushes the reader to supply the missing information from their own understanding of the type of situation. For example, Elizabeth Chadwick's *The Greatest Knight* opens with knights asleep in a hall. This is part of the pageant of the Middle Ages, that is to say, knights and halls are elements of the popular image of the Middle Ages, and she does not need to describe that scene in much detail for the reader to establish where they are and what they think they are seeing.

Another technique is to use the sense of continuity with the present. While this has been mentioned for Mayne's work, it is not an unusual technique. Felicity Pulman uses it when she gives detail of wildlife as her character, Janna, walks through the woods (*Rosemary for Remembrance* opening sequence). The sense of history is given with a wolf's howl, for wolves were made extinct in England from about the thirteenth century. The rural scene both gives a sense of time and connects the reader with it.

Time travel novels carry their own raft of techniques. An important one is the use of the stranger in a strange land, most often the time traveller themselves, for example Penelope in Alison Uttley's *A Traveller in Time*. By making the stranger be such an outsider that she demands or needs explanations in order to function normally within the new environment, Uttley easily and naturally slots into the narrative explanations of what is happening or how things work. The character learns what the reader needs to know, as the reader needs to know it.

Thus, writers often use a voice to shape a belief or an interpretation in the mind of a reader. Someone who is insightful gives an explanation (which can then be trusted), a traveller sees something for the first time, the ignorant is led through an activity for the first time. This is a technique for expressing the world of the novel through the eyes of a particular character. It takes the idea of history in fiction just one step further: the writer is explaining how characters live in the past and is communicating this to the reader. It enables the writer to explore some of the limits of their place and time positively (while fuelling plot and creating narrative complications and tensions for instance) rather than as window dressing.

These representations are not accurate in many cases, and are not supposed to be. They are conventions. This is explored in the work of Stephanie Trigg (see Trigg, 2008: 102, for example).

The world of the novel may be complete in itself (this depends on how it is built) but it is not always consistent with our sense of history. For instance, Connie Willis (1994: 11) has her character realize that 'They were still burning people at the stake in 1320. There was no inoculation to protect her from that or from someone seeing her come through and deciding she was a witch.' In 1320, however, witches were not killed: heretics were. The witch craze had not yet begun in history outside the novel and the first witch trial had barely happened. This does not affect the history within the novel, as long as the reader does not compare Willis' Doomsday history with the history narrated by historians. When the reader makes this comparison, however, the world of the novel is more liable to be perceived as fallible: this is the importance of using telling detail that can be validated against modern historical narratives.

Elana Gomel (2009: 99) suggests that the agency of the narrator and the characters is not the same. The author/narrator contains an open-ended story, but for the characters, the story is complete. This is the power of the character voice in expressing the sense of place time and history within the novel: it is closed, the reader can accept it as historical, even if the bulk of the novel's action is still to come.

Willis (1994: 312) uses the same convention as Uttley (1977) to bring forth emotion. Kivrin in *Doomsday Book* looks around the company and thinks that they are all dead in her time, in the present. This is a technical tool: it delivers the emotional burden of the past and connects the life of the past to the present of the reader. William Mayne does this even more effectively in his novel *Earthfasts*: he uses the idea of history (King Arthur, in this instance as the legendary sleeping king) to connect to a legend. The poetic language is a vehicle that carries the heightened realism and this heightened realism makes the uncanny acceptable. There is very little real historical connection in the novel, but a great deal of emotional connection to the past and to the concept of a continuity of the present with the past. It all comes down to narrative techniques in Mayne's novel, and to a very clever use of telling detail.

Fiction writers use these techniques to create temporal proximity and temporal distance in a not-dissimilar way to historians. Alun Munslow (2011: 11) discusses this as 'duration'. He points out that historians speed up and slow down time through the narration. It is not simply *reported*: it is *managed*, using the tools that help tell the story itself.

The story matters above everything. Genre, being key to the choices the author has in telling their story, also matters. The history that the writer calls upon to perform narrative functions is also critical. There are so many different ways a society can operate and still have most of its members never travel more than a thirty mile radius in their lifetime, for instance. It might be the difference between a housewife on a struggling small property in nineteenth-century outback Australia and a cockney woman in nineteenth-century London: the two woman might be born in the same year and travel the same total distance in their lives and still have hugely different spatial awareness.

Some books are more easily accessible to a wider range of readers because those books have this awareness informing them. The writers either understand space and time and build their world to manifest that clearly (taking this and that, but taking this and that with scrupulous care), or they select very narrow boundaries and stick so closely to those boundaries that the shading of the world of the novel is expressed consistently.

It is inevitable that writers will use their assumptions concerning the past – at least to a degree – as those assumptions are embedded in the creative processes of many writers. However, it must be noted that when historical accounts are presented as truths concerning the past, as correcting the historical record and so on, then writers of fiction have a duty of care to attempt to address these assumptions and misconceptions with the same careful attention that is appropriate to their other work.

***

One element that is absolutely critical to transforming a nebulous notion of the past into an exciting novel is the manner in which the writer translates their research and their conceptualizations into narrative.

In theory, there are two phases to this: conceptualization (world building) and translating (working from story space). In reality, as we have seen, there is only one contiguous space, but it is complex and changes in texture and varies according to the working needs of the writer.

World building can go drastically wrong when the history is poorly understood. For instance, feudal nobles who never who learn anything about war and can be easily defeated creates a plotline where the same events happen over and over, but with no underlying sense of reality causing the repetition. Or a writer may assume that fighting styles are the same across Europe and transpose weaponry and warfare in a way that is not in the least credible. There are several reasons why readers might see this as not real: the same events after the same style over and over might be read as symbolic, for instance. They might be read as leading to violence and the path to violence is no longer anything but a prelude to the real plot. The bottom line is that the perception of functional or real universe becomes a lesser component. This reduces the importance of that perception of reality to the narrative, and therefore diminishes the elements of the world building that contribute to this narrative.

Interestingly, some of these errors are not developed by the writer. They are carried over from the research the writer has done in creating their world. If research into the Middle Ages does not take the writer beyond stock views of chivalry and romantic love, then any historical romance set in the Middle Ages will lack that historical reality. Tom Griffiths points out (2015: 13) that when empathy towards history is called upon without reflection, the way the writer uses history is affected. The stereotypes are popular and thus hard to avoid.

Some writers intentionally do not avoid stereotypes: creating stock romances using stereotypes is to create a saleable work of fiction. This approach is peripheral to this study: due to the nature of the focus group (only one of the authors interviewed writes commercial fiction of this kind), the focus of this book has been on writers who are looking for a sense of historical realism in fiction.

In these novels, it is not just the research that matters, it is its manner and the shape of the intended novel. This is why the foundations of and approach to research are critically important to how the history appears in the final novel: if a writer trusts all non-fiction equally and uncritically, or they develop a single favourite source that simply misinterprets the historical record, or they take single examples of equipment and apply them broadly across different cultures, they create fictional realities that depart significantly from the historical reality. To create a credible history for a place under these conditions takes significantly more sophisticated writing technique than creating a credible history from the current interpretations of historical specialists or from sources that align with the work of current scholarship.

While the focus here is obviously upon history in fiction and thus on worlds for the novel built using known history, this material has a wider significance. Writers who design worlds for novels are better served by dynamic cultures (ones that change over time and operate with a sense of natural movement over time) than by static ones (where the underlying cultural shift is small or non-existent). David Eddings, in his Belgariad series, has created a continent where the cultures are relatively static, for instance. In Eddings' world there are political changes, but they operate in a society that is simplistic and almost in stasis. The inhabitants of each country, therefore, thus develop the appearance of stereotypes after the first volume.

Eddings creates a history without fully understanding the implications of that history. Compare this with Kate Elliott's Cold Magic series, where European history has been carefully extrapolated from a past where Roman domination was quite different in extent and where science operates using different rules.

The difference is in the research that underlies the world building and extrapolation and Elliott's invented world is more sophisticated and subtle and far more dynamic over time. The selection of these two writers was quite intentional, as they represent different ends of the spectrum. Eddings' work appeared in the 1980s and audience demand for a sophisticated and dynamic culture in sequences of fantasy novels was much lower. Furthermore, Elliott is a historian by training, so her fiction has the advantage of higher level research skills and understanding of potential problems as well as a marketplace that accepts a more nuanced and dynamic approach.

Whatever the current reading cultures demand of writers, however, readers live within their cultures. These extremes have not emerged *ex nihilo*, but have arisen from public discourse on what creates a fantasy novel. When a writer lacks advanced training, their first response is often to meet the needs they see in the public responses to current fiction.

Thus some historical fiction currently contains approaches that require these cultural dynamics over time and a sophisticated response to sources and historical research; and some historical fiction does not. Those novels that do, include historical fiction such as that by Elizabeth Chadwick and Sharon Penman (on the 'commercial' side), and historical fiction such as that by Hilary Mantel and Geraldine Brooks (on the 'literary' side). Some speculative fiction falls into this group, too, notably work by authors such as Guy Gavriel Kay and Michael Chabon. Much of the historical romance, for instance, does not require the more sophisticated responses to sources and to historical research, nor does a significant amount of horror. Science fiction is such a mixed genre in this respect that it is hard to categorize. Works such as Jack Dann's *The Memory Cathedral* are sophisticated in their use of history and shifting cultural dynamics; however, overall most other science fiction is less so.

History has its internal dynamic: it is itself a narrative. This means that research is, of itself, not enough. Writers have to either discover a dynamic that is used by historians, or develop one of their own to replace it for the history in the novel to be effective for a wide range of readers.

How does the writer move from the world they have created for their novel into the novel itself? Stephen Jaeger (2011: 34) discusses the movement from the story space or story world into the text itself using textual cues. From a writer's point of view, these cues are straightforward writing techniques or rhetorical devices.

Partly, this can be reduced to whether writers see history (or the history they are researching) as mutable or immutable, as discussed in Chapter 6. Can they change their reading of history for the purposes of the novel? The answers to this were less uniform, in interesting ways.

Elizabeth Chadwick is conscious that her narrative is not going to follow strict historical lines because of her own nature and interests. Her comment in her lack of religious interest and her awareness of its effect on the history she narrates is an excellent example of this. Compare this with Sandra Worth's claim that, 'I honestly try not to alter anything. Even the emotions my characters feet came from what I believe they must have felt, given their physical and emotional makeup, and their situation at the time.' The difference in their approach fits very closely to their approach to the Middle Ages, discussed earlier. The tight emotional link that Worth feels to the period gives her a much closer personal affiliation and means that she lacks the self-awareness that Chadwick possesses and thus interprets her research to meet her heartfelt prior assumptions. Extrapolation from these carefully considered sources is coloured by this view. The narrative is created from the colouring and views, not from the sources. Thus the views writers hold about how mutable history is, are a crucial component in the jigsaw puzzle of how they write history into their fiction.

Brian Wainwright falls clearly into the same camp as Chadwick:

> I try to avoid offending modern sensibilities as far as I can while still retaining the ability to look at myself in the mirror. Medieval people were frequently sexist and xenophobic, loved blood sport, saw nothing wrong in stringing a criminal up from the nearest tree, etc. Above all, the Middle Ages were not a democracy (either in society in general or in the family) and there were very strong class distinctions, social etiquettes, protocols and taboos. I think it is reasonable to tone down some of this, and I often put extreme violence 'off stage'. On the other hand I will not introduce anachronistic political and philosophical opinions – my women are not twenty-first century feminists and the characters are not liberal free thinkers from the eighteenth century Enlightenment.
>
> Some legal and feudal processes are very complex and there are issues it is necessary to simplify in a novel, since one cannot assume all readers have a PhD in Medieval History. Indeed 'simplification' of many aspects is a necessity.

The extent to which writers feel they can modify history is definitely linked to genre. Chadwick, Wainwright and Worth are all historical fiction writers. Dave Luckett – a speculative fiction writer who has written works ranging from fantasy based on medieval society such as *Dark Winter* (1998) to alternate history such as *Subversive Activity* (2009) – has a very different response to that of the historical fiction writers. As has been discussed in Chapter 6, Luckett feels that consistency is important: he is open to changing known history significantly, but within the boundaries of his understanding of human behaviour and institutions. He is one of the minority of writers interviewed who has university-level education in history, so his analysis is based on an understanding of how society operated in standard academic histories concerning the time. His world building is flexible, but he develops a dynamic and credible culture based loosely on the Middle Ages. What he is articulating is not how much 'history' can be changed, however, but that he himself sees that dynamic and is very aware of the need to maintain plausibility in his built world. This is why he began his response with 'any and all' and then modified it. He has strict parameters for changes that can be made, and those parameters are based on his understanding of the Middle Ages.

Of the writers interviewed, Catherine Butler has the most sophisticated awareness of the difference between history and the past. She recognizes the differences between intentional and other changes, and she recognizes the responsibility the writer has to the reader. She explains:

> I haven't [altered history], at least deliberately – except in the trivial sense that this is fiction and therefore not a description of what really happened. As a general question, I'd feel happy altering anything if there was a good reason for it, but I would have to take into account the experience of the noticing and well-informed reader, whom I would prefer not to irritate with pointless inaccuracies.

There is a second group of historical fiction writers who handle the past a little more emotionally, as we have already seen. For instance, Wendy Dunn describes 'the unknowable past. What happens behind closed doors. The emotional journey and growth of historical personages. If there is no way of no knowing, it frees us to be creators by using the framework of history.'

Kathleen Cunningham Guler invents within a carefully considered framework. She expresses herself cautiously. 'Knowingly', in terms of inventing, she would prefer to be able to say that she has done none (that, in an ideal world, she has not invented history):

> ... but I have, both knowingly and unwittingly. Occasionally, I will embellish a detail to enhance a character. For example, I've given my main character, who is a spy, a style of sword that would probably not have existed until a later period, just to make him more 'warrior-like'. (If he's got a better, bigger sword, he can fight harder and longer.) I give the excuse that he is a very clever, inventive man and a blacksmith as well, so he could create his own weapons.

There are differences in the ways historical fiction writers use history, therefore. Maxine McArthur, who has written both space opera and historical fantasy sums up the reason for this variation in approaches: 'Depends on your contract with the reader. If you say you're writing an historical novel, I'd say very few, apart from introducing new characters. If it's an alternate history, the sky's the limit.'

That puts the relationship between history and fiction clearly down to what kind of fiction is being written. This is a wonderful theory, but the reality is more complex. To explore that more complex reality, I asked the writers a follow-up question which has already been discussed in detail and is flagged here because of its importance to the current topic: 'How strong is a writer's responsibility to maintain historical accuracy if he/she uses historical themes?' This question broke down the neatness of the categories. Each writer gave a personal answer. It is from these personal answers that we can see the relationship between the writer and history. The answer to the previous question, it turns out, illuminated the relationship between the writer and the genre they most clearly identify with. It also demonstrated, as we have seen, that the emotive connection that some writers have with history plays a very important part in their work.

A rather important aspect of how writers address history is how they master their source material and transform it into narrative. As discussed earlier, all of them work in stages that indicate an awareness of the need for transformation from source material to the world of the novel, but the stages can be quite different. Elizabeth Chadwick writes a detailed synopsis and adds vast amounts of detail. Both Sandra Worth and Michael Barry have confidence in their relationship with source material. Dave Luckett does not believe that writers actually master source material. This was discussed in Chapter 5. It is intrinsic to how the novel is developed by the writer. Dave Luckett explains:

> [W]e might have to have it acted out for us, the differences between their society and our own. We are used to the idea that wealth and hence elite status consists of ready money; we need it made clear to us in action that, for these people, they consist of control of land. We are used to the idea that children grow up and make their own way; we need it made clear to us that these people are used to the idea that children succeed to their parents' occupation, but that three in ten of them won't grow up at all.
>
> Those are the important things to understand. There aren't so many of them, really.

The crux is that the writer needs to understand the history they use from a point of view that works for their story. Without that understanding, the story fails. Felicity Pulman's sophisticated awareness of her relationship with the material she uses highlights this:

> For me, writing is quite an intuitive, unconscious sort of process. Primarily, I think of the story, or part of it, or I become interested in a character and a situation, and then I look for the facts and do the research to back it up (e.g. legend, or time and location, or historic events, much as I've described above). This information, in turn,

often suggests other story possibilities, and it becomes a circular sort of process. So I research as I go, but mostly I focus on writing the story. So far as dialogue is concerned, I 'hear' my characters speaking, and reproduce what they say, hoping that it isn't too anachronistic. I am fearful of a consciously academic approach to writing my stories because I know that it would inhibit the creative flow. As you probably realise, I'd rather tell the story first and then either change it or manipulate the facts to fit.

The authors vary considerably in their access to formal literary definitions and their interest in such definitions. The writer who defines herself most clearly in terms of the academy, Robyn Starkey (who has a strong background in literary history) was most careful not to use words with too great a literary loading in describing her own work. Other writers have little or nothing to do with the academy, save that they might be studied by literary experts. The link with formal genre study is therefore at best nebulous, at worst entirely irrelevant.

Most of the writers can group into one of two broad genre classifications according to the terms they use to describe their own fiction. Writers who define themselves as writing fantasy or high fantasy include Chris Andrews, Catherine Butler, Ross Hamilton, Dave Luckett, Sophie Masson, Sally Odgers and Maxine McArthur. Writers who define themselves as writing historical fiction or romantic historical include Elizabeth Chadwick, Wendy J. Dunn, Helen Hollick, Debra A. Kemp, Brian Wainwright and Sandra Worth. These are the two poles, and the writing at each end is quite distinctive. As an aside, it can also be observed that writers who have also written speculative fiction (Barry, Andrews, Butler, Luckett, Odgers in particular) are likely to cite purely technical reasons as underlying their use of history and are also most likely to respond to history as a technical aid to their writing rather than as something they passionately explore.

Different narrative techniques are used by writers at each end of the pole: the historical end, for instance, emphasizes authenticity and the reality of the past. There is more quest adventure in the fantasy end and more focus on personal development by the romance/historical writers. This difference almost always carries through to the narratorial voice and even to the publisher's presentation of the novel. The author's genre descriptions show us a great deal about modern genre fiction writing.

It also fits with what we have seen concerning the author's identification with the subject of their novel: where a writer describes themselves as writing due to historical fascination, they are more likely to be passionately drawn to it and also to define themselves as writing historical fiction. Kemp and Worth, for example, have strong emotional affiliations with the historical places and times in which they set their fiction. The feeling in reading the self-descriptions of these writers is that a period (in the former, the Early Middle Ages and in the latter the later Middle Ages) may be important in and of itself, and not merely brought into the novel for technical reasons. This may be particularly true with certain themes, especially Richard III (Worth) and Arthur (Kemp) although the sample of writers is too small to do more than suggest this might be so.

The function that history serves in the work thus has a strong bearing on the most appropriate techniques and the quality of the work within its own genre often depends on an appropriate choice of techniques. The techniques the writer deploys has an important relationship with both the strength of the narrative overall and with the validation of the history within the tale.

CHAPTER 9

The writer's relationship with narrative: Tools and techniques

What has emerged in the course of this study is that writers' relationships with their narrative are important to understanding how writers position the history in their work. This chapter focuses on the narrative itself. It presents a 'novelist's skills audit' that helps elucidate further the writer's relation with the narrative and what tools writers use to introduce their particular narrative to the reader and help form the reader's expectations. This includes some discussion of how writers indicate genre at the beginning of a work; in other words, some of the means by which writers indicate to readers the path that the readers should expect the narrative will travel. It also examines how writers use specific constructs (including ones that indicate a sense of place and time) to create bridges between the reader and the narrative. This chapter examines why stylistic choices assist the writer in communicating both history and story to the reader.

All historical narratives are interpretative acts; that is, all historical narratives create a relationship between the reader and the past. Novels that incorporate history are interpretative acts that include choices of form as well as choices of content and style. If the story focuses on politics and military strategy, the language is likely to be spare, for instance, and descriptions of clothes are likely to focus on elements that suggest rank. The choices of detail a writer makes are key to understanding how history is incorporated into their work, but also ways in which a novel suggests to readers how to interpret the work itself and, by implication, the history within it.

When a writer decides to incorporate history in their fiction, this has flow-on effects on the other choices they make. Their interpretative act is different, in other words, from the way it would be if history were not intentionally included. The difference between a writer saying 'an adult woman' and 'an adult woman wearing a slightly soiled wimple' is significant: the former leaves the reader to fill in traits of what they consider to be an adult woman and the latter not only gives a standard medieval construction for an adult woman (for adult women wore wimples) but presents an indication of the woman's personality through the appearance of that wimple. These choices can help indicate genre. Telling detail that is more precise in historical terms (the wimple) is more likely to indicate historical fiction.

The specific elements that a writer must consider in order to successfully incorporate history in their fiction along genre lines thus need to be addressed. Considering these elements amounts to a 'skills audit' for the writer who wants to write genre successfully.

Writer's skills audit

Four basic components will be discussed:

1) genre indicators
2) writer identification of audience needs
3) methods of explaining technical matter
4) where material comes from and how it is assimilated

1. Genre indicators

Genre indicators tell the reader what to expect. Without initial and terminal genre indicators, readers have no guidelines to assess where to place a novel and what narrative expectations they ought to have.

The opening of a novel is possibly the single most important element in this respect, for it is usually where genre is suggested to the reader most clearly. Openings might suggest stories of quite different kinds, for instance a fantasy/folk world that is close to ours in nature (Sophie Masson's *Scarlet in the Snow* [2013]), compared with an otherworld gritty past (Joe Abercrombie *Half the World* [2015]).

Here is Sophie Masson's opening to *Scarlet in the Snow*:

> Three sisters sat spinning at the old tower window, watching for their mother to come home. After a time the first sister said, 'I see our mother's sleigh, flying through the forest, laden with fine things, with silks and satins, velvets and furs.' Then the second sister said, 'I see our mother's sleigh speeding over snowy fields, laden with valuable things, with caskets of jewels, pearls and amber and gold.'

This opening is of a character writing a story, and the story is clearly a fairy tale. The three sisters spinning and their dreams about their mother demonstrate the key words and also show the boundaries of the story, which is a retelling of *Beauty and the Beast*. The yearning for their mother implied in the opening is the emotion that draws the reader in and the fairy tale is what the reader should hope to find within the book, given the opening.

Here is Joe Abercrombie's opening to *Half the World*:

> He hesitated just an instant, but long enough for Thorn to club him in the balls with the rim of her shield.
>
> Even over the racket of the other lads all baying for her to lose, she heard Brand groan.

The violence in the first sentence, combined with names such as Thorn and Brand, is a clarion call for epic fantasy. The fact that Thorn is both female and an underdog (for the watchers are 'baying for her to lose') sets up the emotion: readers are pushed towards supporting her. That the fight is neither gentlemanly or terribly fair (since Brand has been hit in the balls) suggests gritty fantasy.

Openings bear a high number of audience indicators and genre markers, for they are the point of entry for most readers. An excellent opening will engage the reader from several directions at once. It will introduce characters, voice, story, and give a clear indication of the genre. This is why, of all the aspects of the author's toolkit, openings are most critical to the understanding of *history* in fiction. It is the opening of a novel that indicates to the reader what level and kind of history to expect in the novel. Look again at the openings of the two works mentioned.

Sophie Masson's opening places its readers in a historical past (not yet revealed as fantasy-based history) through the use of spinning. That it is not a medieval setting is suggested by the age of the tower window they are looking through. That it is not a modern novel is suggested by the sleigh. By situating the novel in time through technology (spinning and the sleigh) and through the building (a tower suggests a castle, an old tower suggests a more modern tale that has an old backdrop) Masson gives a strong historical background for her story without using too much detail.

In Joe Abercrombie's opening to *Half the World* the shield serves a similar function to the spinning and the sleigh. The action narrative and the potential for real damage intimates to the reader that this is serious, that it, that we are not reading about a student fight using ancient techniques.

In 2006 (12 August, ASiF) as part of a series of online interviews, I outlined a series of ideas and notions that writers might indicate through openings:

1) addressing the precise target audience
2) choosing subjects that fall within the boundaries of the genre and, if the key subjects in the novel fall outside (a historical quest fantasy that is based in suburban Cleveland, for instance) then the opening is a key opportunity for convincing readers that boundary-shift is essential
3) the writer might explain that there is a tale that needs to be told and what other tales fit in the same lines. This is a call to attention and it indicates clearly that the theme the audience wants to read is the one the novel addresses. These are the chief selling points for the novel proper
4) using key words that indicate what kind of variant of a common tale this narrative is. 'Elflord' for Tolkien-derived fantasy, for example, or words associated with archery for a story that draws on Robin Hood legends.

All of these techniques help delineate the type of history in the novel, but they also suggest potential reader interpretations. A more complex opening implies that the readers ought to become involved in a different manner to a simpler opening. It develops quite different explanations of history in fiction than those novels where the action begins instantly. The history is used in both action based fiction and fiction focussed on character development, but it is used in quite specific ways. The opening signals to readers that this will happen. Sitting in a tower room suggests that private lives are more likely to be the focus of a story, while being hit in the balls by a shield suggests that action takes precedence. It is not an absolute demarcation: action-based stories can still have strong characterization and story arcs for characters and character based stories are still able to have much action. It is relative, signalled to the readers at the commencement of the tale.

The exception to this is a long series of linked works created by the one author. The worlds of Raymond Feist, or the worlds created and explored by Roger Zelazny's Amber princes need not rely as much on their openings (although Feist relies on more normative genre openings and writing style than does Zelazny) for a major component of their audience consists of readers who already know the premises of their stories. This reduces the readers' need for explanations due to the familiarity of the setting, but it does not actually change how history functions in the novel.

Looking at this from a slightly different direction, the opening paragraphs of a novel 'sell' the work to readers. In doing this, in indicating genre and style, the writer treats the reader as assuming that the novel will meet the expectations set up by those initial words. In the case of history in fiction, this is the key point in the novel where the writer sets up expectations for the level and nature of history in the novel.

In *Pasquale's Angel* (1994) Paul McAuley opens with a precisely delineated, technically considered view of the past:

> Morning. Just after Dawn. The sky, for once clear of the murk spewed by foundries and manufactories, the rich blue of the very best four-florins-to-the-ounce ultramarine. Dyers, leather-aproned, long gloves sling around their necks, hair brushed back and tucked under leather caps.

Soon the reader will be presented with information that irrefutably establishes an alternate history setting, with the Industrial Revolution happening in sixteenth-century Florence. To achieve a successful alternate history McAuley uses richness of detail, so that his new history can be reconciled with known history. It is this richness of detail that marks the novel's opening. By creating parallels between the colour of the sky and industry and linking these clearly to commerce, some of the major concerns of the novel are linked to the culture and the place and the period (mercantile Florence, in hour own historical timeline; mercantile and industrial Florence in McAuley's) and the role history will play in this work is made clear.

Philippa Gregory opens *The White Queen* (2009) somewhat differently. She uses a prologue, indicating to the reader that the first page is apart from the main narrative but explanatory of it, and that prologue begins:

> In the darkness of the forest the young knight could hear the splashing of the fountain long before he could see the glimmer of moonlight reflected on the still surface.

The fairytale atmosphere of the prologue, added to the appearance of a knight in a forest, suggests that the pageantry of the Middle Ages will be drawn upon for this novel. Thus, despite the post-prologue novel-proper beginning 'My father is Sir Richard Woodville, Baron Rivers ...' and a concrete past-as-given-by historians is suggested, the prologue adds a layer. Gregory is suggesting to her readers that the history she presents is both accurate ('Sir Richard Woodville, Baron Rivers' is concrete detail and undeniable as a personal identification) and romantic. The concluding lines of the prologue suggest that the tale will be a tragic one. These signals are suggestions from the writer that the story should be read as larger than life, as fabulous, as a bit mysterious, and that the history is a detailed setting for grandeur.

There are a thousand ways of opening a novel, and each of them gives the reader a sense of what to expect. By embedding the type of historical interpretation ('not our world' in McAuley's, 'legendary' in Gregory's) each writer demonstrates how they intend to translate their history into fiction for their readers.

2. Writer identification of audience needs

How writers identify audience needs is a vexed and complicated question. It emerges as an issue chiefly because writers allude to it. For instance, in a group discussion with Geoff Ryman at an online science fiction convention (Flycon, 2009), where he spoke freely about his work with his readers, Ryman mentioned that his agent suggested he write a different type of work to his previous books. The inherent implication was that by changing style and theme he could then meet audience needs and that he would sell more books.

Within my reference group and wider writing circles, very few emerging and established writers pay no attention to audience at all. Writers such as Trudi Canavan and Elizabeth Chadwick have active correspondence with their readers, and Elizabeth Chadwick maintains a lively conversation with her readers through social media websites such as Facebook and Twitter. However, within my writing classes and the classes of other teaching writers, novices often admit they have not yet established an audience and therefore are their own first and second opinion. These differences do not only indicate difference in writers' awareness of their audience and the needs of their audience, and shifting levels of sophistication in these matters according to career position; they may also indicate that some writers develop audiences because of shared interests that are expressed through the writing.

Writers do not merely identify with an audience or consult with an audience or suspect that a particular readership will be interested in their fiction: they actively think about what that readership may want. The smallest readership that can be found in an audit of writers' skills is one person: the writer themselves. Authors such as George R. R. Martin, Stephenie Meyer and J. K. Rowling have too many readers to connect very closely thus, for these writers, most of their audience's relationship with them is solely through the book.

Readers are more likely to develop active engagement with fellow fans than with the writer. Elizabeth Chadwick, for instance, has a following of around 3,500 active readers on one of her social media pages (Facebook). A core of about forty of them interact with her on a regular basis. In her answers to the questions concerning her audience, however, Chadwick (as we have already seen) admits that she writes primarily to please herself. This suggests that for her, at least, the needs of readers and author probably overlap due to shared interests. As well as her personal Facebook page, for example, she manages a page dedicated to the history of William Marshall, and a number of her fans contribute to both. She is, however, one case only, and her readers may interact with her quite differently in different forums, and it is possible that her work is indeed influenced by them but that the questions she was asked did not reflect this influence. This example demonstrates that audience is not simple to define and that the answers the writers gave concerning who they write for may differ depending on context, but the broader question of how readers interact with writers and what insights writers gain from these interactions is unfortunately a question beyond the scope of this study. It is important, nevertheless, that it be raised: the nature of relationships between writers and their readers/audiences is a substantial question for writers.

3. Methods of explaining technical matter

In any novel there is a certain amount of background material that must be communicated to the reader. The level of technicality and the amount of material depends very much on the genre and so does the preferred method of communicating it. While this is common to novel writing in general, writers of speculative fiction often describe this as 'info-dumping', which is useful as an indication that the tools writers use vary from one type of novel to another. Info-dumping is a term used to explain how explanations of the background necessary to understand the novel overwhelm the plot and characters. The style of presentation of technical and descriptive matter in a novel is genre related.

There are various writing techniques that enable background material to be inserted into a novel. Key methods of conveying information include:

a)   Technical description embedded into plot devices
b)   Descriptions or blocks of information
c)   Snippets of information incorporated into the text (telling detail).

a)   Technical description embedded into plot devices

Technical matter can be presented in several ways, but is most noticeable when it is presented as solid blocks of substance. This is obtrusively noticeable because solid blocks of substance can destabilize plot and character, that is to say, they can obstruct the progression of the narrative.

Where the technical matter is essential to understand the plot, a detailed description can be woven into the narrative without destabilizing effect by using forms familiar within the genre of the novel. For example in Michael Crichton's *Timeline*, the time machine needs to be credible. Although Crichton was writing an action thriller, he needed a strong level of technical description of his time machine to set up the danger and the impossible situation that needed resolving. To achieve this, he has a character view the machine for the first time and see its newness and inexplicability. Wonder and surprise at new technology is a common device in science fiction, allowing technical descriptions that do not disrupt the flow of the narrative. From this moment of wonder, it is this character's growing understanding of the machine that leads the reader through the dense technical prose. Scott Baker in *The Rule of Knowledge* (2013) similarly integrates a significant amount of material through having a key character discover his own future. In both instances, it is how a character learns that enables the writer to incorporate densely informative material as an integral part of the narrative. This technique enables the writers to develop action sequences that involve characters using or misusing the machine. Without this explanation, the disruptions to the body that travel in time created would have lacked impact.

The question is not how much extraneous matter is incorporated into a novel, therefore, but whether the writer has the skills to handle it within their genre and what techniques they employ.

b) Descriptions or blocks of information

There are many methods of incorporating blocks of text that convey a substantial amount of information to the reader. For instance, a significant quantity of explanation and back story can be incorporated into the narrative proper as an explanation from one character to another, or as a text the character reads. Rather than showing a character dying, for instance, their daughter may read a letter that says, 'My dear daughter, your father's death was unseemly. He died at his club at four in the morning from a surfeit of port and laudanum.' When the information is brief, it simply informs the current line of action and is not, therefore, info-dumping. If the letter were to ramble for two pages containing much detail about a death that was of minimal relevance to plot and to character development, then it could be considered info-dumping.

We have already encountered info-dumping as the extreme example of delivering blocks of information in a story, where the blocks do not carry the plot or characters forward and thus push the main narrative aside. This can happen when a block of text develops from an informative expansion on the subject at a suitable moment. If a character was riding past a house and there were, for example, several paragraphs concerning the architecture of the house and its inhabitants and this information was not linked closely to the character observing the house or the usual voice and level of detail given by the narrator, then this could be considered info-dumping.

Critically, the nature of info-dumping is not consistent across genres. In fact, some genres allow (or even require) writing that would, in another genre, be regarded as info-dumping.

Info-dumping is not simply conveying detail within a story. There are many techniques for conveying information about background to a story. As we have seen, the only techniques that genuinely dump information are ones that deliver large slabs of information in such a way that the tale is delayed or diverted, that is to say where the information is delivered in such a way as to disrupt or overwhelm the narrative.

'Overwhelm' relates to genre and its norms: acceptable levels of detail in one novel are not acceptable in another. In Michael Chabon's *The Yiddish Policeman's Union* (2007) there are considerable descriptions of the invented city where the action takes place: these descriptions are generally within the bounds for a detective novel set in an exotic location with an exotic culture. Anne Bishop, on the other hand, also uses an exotic setting. Her novels are of an entirely different genre, however, being dark fantasy (often describes as 'romantic fantasy'). She provides a great deal of background to her built world and it does not always advance the plot. In her more recent novels, the background has become stronger and may be seen by some readers as overwhelming. This is because her work is clearly fantasy, which has an imperative for plot advancement through action and through characterization, and a lower tolerance than some genres for a body of information in a block in the text proper. These blocks of background are less of a problem for readers of most hard science fiction (for example, the work of Stephen Baxter or Isaac Asimov). Hard science fiction, with its focus on exploring technical questions concerning humans and the universe, has a higher tolerance for background or informative description.

c) Telling detail, snippets of information incorporated into the text

Telling detail is a common technique used by writers to incorporate historical information into a story, as discussed earlier. A tiny piece of information can indicate the historical world the characters live in while adding to the characterization and even the plot.

Kathleen Cunningham Guler illustrates this in her discussion of how she builds dialogue in her fiction:

> With dialog, in any historical novel, the author walks a tightrope. In writing of post-Roman Britain, I have chosen to use speech that is smooth and natural but not modern sounding. It cannot sound too archaic, otherwise it will be stilted and offend the reader. I've taken the tack that out of the old Brythonic language many dialects have developed by the latter half of the fifth century. This shows the beginning of the gradual shift into Old Welsh and Old Cornish and so on. (Of course the characters don't know that will happen.) Higher-ranking characters speak Latin, because of the lingering Roman influence. The various Germanic languages are also recognized in Saxon/Anglo/Jutish characters. Occasionally I work in an actual word or phrase here and there for effect as long as it is clear of the meaning through the story.

Once Guler has finished this background work, all that is visible is the speech of the characters. The speech cannot be extracted as an example, for, as she describes, it applies to the whole: she is after a general effect. She gives that overall effect a particular character, however, through her use of the occasional word or phrase. Those words or phrases are her telling detail, to indicate precisely when and where the speech of those characters belong.

Another use of telling detail is to present a character or a scene and to illuminate it and give it depth. Sharon Kay Penman's *When Christ and His Saints Slept* (1995) uses telling detail extensively, for this very reason. Penman presents small details of historical norms as part of the development of character or plot, thus reinforcing the history in the novel as an integral part of the novel itself and of her writing style. For example, one character looks across at another and thinks 'She was getting too old to wear her hair loose like that.' It reinforces the relationship between the two characters while intimating that, in the twelfth century, adult women generally wore their hair covered.

4. Where material comes from and how it is assimilated

Any writer needs to understand the difference between borrowing, adaptation and appropriation. Where the built world comes from and whether it is assimilated or acknowledged and used sensitively is something all writers have to face.

The complexity of the work involved in writing a story helps explain the relationship between fiction writers and the work of historians. The story can mimic the role of the historian, articulating and annotating it. It can also have a much looser attachment (sometimes none at all) with the work of the historian. The claims of research made by the writer are not directly connected to these choices. For example, Guy Gavriel Kay uses (consciously) material that is not contemporaneous to his novels, explaining that 'I spin fantasies upon themes of history' (Auden, n.d.). Furthermore, what many novelists think of as 'correct history' is in many cases not the same as the historian's perception. This has already been discussed.

***

The writer's toolbox, when used properly, incorporates the history that works for that particular novel into the writer's fiction. Once the work is complete, the dialogue is between the book and its readers. The readers are in story space and responsible for their own interpretations.

This is quite different to the historian's relationship with historical narratives for the historian is in a constant dialogue with sources and in additional constant dialogues with other historians: their story space can be quite specific to their work. Historians discuss this frequently, expressing concerns about even the most precise historical fiction. For instance on the anonymous blog titled 'Magistra et Mater' (2009), the historian who owns the blog explains the discomfort she feels on reading historical fiction: 'The two things I find suspension of disbelief killers are anachronisms in dialogue and social attitudes.' She discusses her increased sensitivity as she moved from being a lay reader into being a professional historian reading novels. Many historians look for the codes that they know will reassure them, and those codes do not necessarily match those in the author's toolkit. The author's toolkit, in other words, may help present history in fiction, but the presentation is intended for general audiences as a rule, not for historians.

***

As John Tosh and Sean Lang say (while discussing the nature of historical writing, not fiction): 'it is not enough to invoke the past; there must also be a belief that getting the story right matters' (2006: 2).

Genre cannot be ignored as a factor in this. Classic science fictional settings, for instance, with their assumption that they are fuelled by an underlying 'What if?' question push them from the fictional to the meta-fictional. We saw this earlier, when discussing Maxine McArthur's Japanese setting. This is true even when that assumption is poorly realized or not realized at all. The story cannot be assumed to be real, but only possible. At its best it tests our reality and our understandings (for instance in Ian McDonald's *Brasyl* [2007]), and at its worst leaves a smug assumption that these understandings are tested.

History within this type of novel is a little different to history within most other novels: by demonstrating the illusion of fiction, a path is opened for discussing the history within it. It can be done within literary novels as well (the common element is metafiction) as well, for instance in the alternate endings John Fowles provides for *The French Lieutenant's Woman* or the first person narrative provides in Hilary Mantel's Cromwell books.

Essentially, the departure from the normative ways of writing history into fiction opens this door to metafiction and to questioning the role of history in fiction. This has a major impact on how we interpret the comments by writers concerning their interest in putting history in fiction. The use of metafiction and questioning the role of history in fiction is not, however, a standard aspect of most fiction that incorporates history. In fact, the majority of science fictional novels do not even begin to question the role of history in fiction or how we access our past through our fiction, but the strength of the science fiction base is that it is possible, just as the strength of literary fiction is that it is possible. Of the writers originally questioned, the only one who expressed a (mild) history of metafiction in the interviews was Chaz Brenchley, although Catherine Butler and Robyn Starkey are also literary scholars and quite possibly use their academic writings to open a discourse in these directions. This suggests that although the metafictional possibilities of science fiction and literary fiction create the possibility of a self-awareness and a more complex understanding of history that adds layers to the emotions and approaches discussed with the interviewees, only a small percentage of writers actually explore these possibilities. In the science fictional world, this includes writers such as Paul McAuley (for instance, *Pasquale's Angel* [1995]) and Jack Dann (for instance, *The Rebel* [2004]).

Other types of novelists look at history in a created past. They argue using the plot, characterization and, most importantly the world-build, but they argue about the interpretation of the past or how we interpret the history that is already part of our cultural backgrounds. These types permit broader questions to be advanced under the umbrella of fiction.

Fantasy fiction covers such a wide spectrum that it can participate from either end: the metafictional or the more literal narrative. Guy Gavriel Kay explains (2005):

> I'm fascinated by both the way in which the past is so different from today *and* by how similar it is in other ways. They 'do things differently there' but at the same time (so to speak), 'Tho' much is taken, much abides.' At times the expectation of difference misleads us. There was, for example, a fairly recent, very strong fashion among historians to assume parents didn't care much about their children in medieval times (high mortality rates, too many kids, etc.). Most of the recent data and research suggests that this is untrue.
>
> I'm intrigued by all issues of this sort. I also find fantasy as a method to be exceptionally useful – a prism of sorts for addressing these matters. It removes a level of presumption, that we can *know* what Justinian and Theodora's marriage was like, or grasp the 'true' religious world-view of someone in the British Isles in the 9th century. Fantasy offers an up-front acknowledgement of the guesswork and imagination involved, frees author and reader (to my mind) from some moral and intellectual traps.

The writers' toolkit is universal, but each writer uses it in their own way.

Conclusion

The relationship between history and fiction is complex, and looking for understanding from a new direction – through discussion with writers about their own work – has led to some very interesting conclusions. The key conclusion is that writers place history in the service of story. The type of story is critical to how history is used in fiction, and the nature of the writer's interest in story influences the type of story chosen.

Within this framework, history plays an important role in building the world of the novel and in helping the writer advance the story. History has roles both in world building and in narrative and these roles vary from writer to writer. Thus history is always at the service of story (and when this relationship is broken, info-dumping ensues and the narrative falters), but in story's service, it does not always serve the same function.

The writing techniques used by fiction writers are tools that demonstrate the importance of specific aspects of narrative that structure the narrative for the reader, that create bridges between reader and narrative, that present voice (whether the narrator's or that of characters in the novel), and that demonstrate the stylistic choices the writer has made in order to define their narrative. These are the tools that enable the writer's narrative. History is in service, therefore, to a series of techniques that are in turn in service to the story.

The relationship of the writer with their story and the use of history within this helps explain the techniques writers use to research and to construct their world, but it also helps explain the relationships writers have with historians. All types of historical research, whether they require sources or asking questions of historians, are at the service of the story being told. This is why some writers ask historians to 'fact check' when, from the viewpoint of the historian, the underlying fabric of history is false, not merely the historical data being checked. Historians and fiction writers do not have parallel narratives, in other words; they have significantly different narratives that may touch in places.

There is also a significant difference between writers of historical fiction and of speculative fiction. Their attitudes towards history are often expressed differently and they will also use history quite differently to each other. The simple fact is that fiction writers write to contemporary narrative norms. They use material to validate their approach and to illuminate the period and place: this material is used in various ways in their work, most notably as telling detail that highlights and helps the story without impeding it through excessive information. When fiction writers call on historical fact to validate their work through using it as telling detail, they are not drawing on the actual past as it happened, for, as we have seen, it is irretrievable. What they draw on is illustrative detail from other narratives. Sometimes these narratives are the work of historians, sometimes they come from memory or from primary sources.

Along the road to understanding the complexity of the writing process and how it uses history, there were some interesting vistas. Writers are strongly individual, and their processes are less shared than overlapping. Likewise, the definitions that writers provide of their own work are not necessarily close or similar to those provided by scholars and audiences. Overall, speculative fiction writers were more likely to take more liberties with the historical side of the narrative than historical fiction writers. Historical fiction writers are more likely to use the history for emotive reasons. Genre reflects the underlying feelings and understanding that writers have concerning their work and the decisions they make concerning it. These are not clinical choices: they reflect the writer's personality and interests.

There is a strong link between self-definition of genre by the writer and the feeling that the past is mutable or immutable. There is also a strong link between genre and the level of research and historical articulation. The emotive link with the historical setting appears stronger in most writers of 'historical' work. How the author defines his or her genre will usually have a significant impact on their relationship with history.

Inevitably, the research undertaken for this book has also opened the door to further questions that need answering.

First, is the link between history and genre unique to history or does it apply to other areas of academic study that are used in building the world of the novel? How far do the conclusions reached here, for instance, apply to anthropology or to geology? Is history a special case, or do the insights gained from this study also represent the relationship between fiction writers and other areas of scholarship?

Second, a major factor in the finished book intervenes after the writer has finished their work and is accepted for publication. What roles do the processes of publishing and the culture of publishing and the politics of publicising play in the final novel? How far is the author's intention (as expressed in these interviews) displayed in different types of novels for different types of markets?

Third, of course, is the importance of genre. The focus of this study was on speculative fiction and historical fiction, with some discussion of literary fiction. Can the results from this study be applied to other long prose fiction? Can it be applied to short prose fiction, or to poetry? What about the narratives maintained through games and through movies and other media? Some of the research holds for writers of short fiction (for several of the writers interviewed also write short fiction) but is this true more generally? In other words, how far do the conclusions reached in this study apply across English language narrative culture?

Finally, if we cannot know how far the conclusions apply to different narratives, we also cannot know how far it represents English language culture as a whole. This study was focussed on certain regions. It only included one non-native English speaker from outside the English-speaking world (Aliette de Bodard, who nevertheless writes in English) and the interviewees came from Australia, the UK, the USA and Canada. How valid are the conclusions for the rest of the English speaking world? How valid are they for the same genres of writing outside the English language?

Furthermore, the study was unable to examine the cultural differences within the target groups, as the numbers of interviewees were insufficient to illuminate whether, for example, a Welsh background produced cultural expectations about novels which were quite different from the cultural expectations of those with a Western Australian background.

This study, then, answered many questions, but it also set up questions that still need answering, particularly concerning the effects on the published novel of the cultures of the writing world and the cultures that writers inhabit. It establishes a framework, however, from which further questions can be answered and more insights gained into how fiction operates within its cultural contexts and what dynamics it wields as an element of culture. It helps us understand how novels – in particular, historical fiction and speculative fiction – each uses history in different ways to achieve story.

Historical fantasy and historical fiction rest upon a shared view of the past, and the narrative is strengthened by the use of history. History, therefore, becomes a tool for use within story space, to add meaning to the narrative.

Bibliography

Abercrombie, Joe, *Half the World* (London: HarperCollins, 2015).

Abercrombie, Joe, *The Heroes* (London: Gollancz, 2012).

Abnett, Dan, *Triumff* (Nottingham: Angry Robot, 2009).

Alter, Robert, *Partial Magic: the Novel as a Self-Conscious Genre* (Berkeley: University of California Press, 1975).

Ankersmit, Frank, 'Truth in History and Literature', *Narrative* 18: 1 (2010), 29–50.

Auden, Sandy, 'Historical Significance: An Interview with Guy Gavriel Kay', <http://www.infinityplus.co.uk/nonfiction/intggk.htm> accessed 15 May 2013.

Auden, Sandy, 'A Question of Character. An Interview with Guy Gavriel Kay', *SFSite* (2005), <https://www.sfsite.com/04b/sagk198.htm> accessed 15 May 2013.

Auerbach, E., *Mimesis: The Representation of Reality in Western Literature*, tr. W.R. Trask. (New York: Doubleday, 1957).

Australian Speculative Fiction in Focus (ASiF), Discussion Forum, <http://pandora. nla.gov.au/pan/122762/20100929–0816/www.asif.dreamhosters.com/forum/index.html> accessed 10 December 2006

Avery, Fiona, *The Crown Rose* (Amherst: Pyr, 2005).

Bacon-Smith, Camille, *Science Fiction Culture* (Philadelphia: University of Pennsylvania Press, 1999).

Baigent, Michael, Richard Leigh and Henry Lincoln, *Holy Blood, Holy Grail* (New York: Dell, 1983).

Baker, Scott, *The Rule of Knowledge* (Sydney: Hachette Australia, 2013).

Barr, Marleen S., *Alien to Femininity: Speculative Fiction and Feminist Theory* (Westport, CT: Greenwood, 1987).

Barthelme, Donald, *The King* (New York: Harper & Row, 1990).

Baumgarten, M., 'The Historical Novel: Some Postulates', *CLIO* 4 (1975), 173–81.

Bergonzi, B., 'Fictions of History', *The Contemporary English Novel*. ed. E. Karl (London: E. Arnold, 1979), 42–65.

Bloch, Marc, *Feudal Society, Volumes 1–2*, tr. L.A. Manyon. (Chicago: University of Chicago Press, 1961–5).

Bould, Mark, Andrew M. Butler, Adam Roberts and Sherryl Vint, eds, *The Routledge Companion to Science Fiction* (London and New York: Routledge, 2009).

Bourin, Monique, 'L'historiographie du marché de la terre au moyen age dans la France meridionale', *Le marché de la terre au moyen age*, eds Laurent Feller and Chris Wickham (Rome: Ecole Francaise de Rome, 2005), 131–45.

Brenchley, Chaz, *Tower of the King's Daughter* (London: Orbit, 1998).

Brown, Dan, *The Da Vinci Code* (New York: Anchor, 2006).

Bunyan, John, *Pilgrim's Progress* (Oxford and New York: Oxford University Press, 2003).

Butler, Charles, *The Lurkers* (London: HarperCollins Children's, 2006).

Byatt, A.S., *On Histories and Stories: Selected Essays* (Cambridge, MA: Harvard University Press, 2001).

Canary, Robert H., and Henry Kozicki, eds, *The Writing of History: Literary Form and Historical Understanding* (Madison: University of Wisconsin Press, 1978).

Canavan, Trudi, *Thief's Magic* (London: Orbit, 2014).

Carr, E.H., *What is History?* (New York: Penguin Books, 1961; 2nd edn, 1987).

Carter, Jonathan A., 'Telling Times: History, Emplotment, and Truth', *History and Theory* 42 (2003), 1–27.

Chabon, Michael, *Gentlemen of the Road* (London: Sceptre, 2007).

Chabon, Michael, *The Yiddish Policeman's Union* (London: Harper Perennial, 2008).

Chadwick, Elizabeth, *The Greatest Knight. William Marshall: A Novel of a Legendary Man* (London: Time Warner Books, 2005).

Chandler, Daniel (1997): 'An Introduction to Genre Theory' [WWW document], <http://www.aber.ac.uk/media/Documents/intgenre/chandler_genre_theory.pdf> accessed 21 February 2014

Clarke, Susanna, *Jonathan Strange and Mr Norrell* (London: Bloomsbury, 2004).

Clendinnen, Inga, 'Fellow Sufferers: History and Imagination', *Australian Humanities Review* (September 1996), <http://www.lib.latrobe.edu.au/AHR/archive/Issue-Sept-1996/clendinnen.html> accessed 12 June 2012.

Clendinnen, Inga, 'The History Question: Who Owns the Past?', *Quarterly Essay* 23 (2006), 1–72.

Cohn, Dorrit, *The Distinction of Fiction* (Baltimore, MD: The Johns Hopkins University Press, 2000).

Cooper, Susan, *The Dark is Rising* (London: Chatto & Windus, 1973).

Cornwall, Bernard, *Harlequin* (London: HarperCollins, 2000).

Courtney, Bryce, *The Potato Factory* (Melbourne: Penguin Australia, 1995)

Cowart, David, *History and the Contemporary Novel* (Carbondale and Edwardsville, IL: Southern Illinois University Press, 1989)

Crichton, Michael, *Timeline* (London: Random House, 1999).

Csicsery-Ronay, Istvan, Jr., *The Seven Beauties of Science Fiction* (Middletown, CT: Wesleyan University Press, 2008).

Curthoys, Ann, and John Docker, *Is History Fiction?* (Sydney: University of NSW Press, 2005. Second edition 2010).

Dann, Jack, *The Rebel: An Imagined Life of James Dean* (New York: William Morrow, 2004).

Dann, Jack. *The Memory Cathedral: A Secret History of Leonardo da Vinci* (New York, Bantam Books, 1995)

Darville/Demidenko, Helen, *The Hand that Signed the Paper* (Sydney: Allen and Unwin, 1994)

de Bodard, Aliette, *Servant of the Underworld* (Nottingham: Angry Robot, 2010).

de Groot, Jerome, *The Historical Novel* (London and New York: Routledge, 2010).

De Mey, Tim, and Erik Weber, 'Explanation and Thought Experiments in History', *History and Theory* 42 (2003), 28–38.

Dening, Greg, *Mr Bligh's Bad Language: Passion, Power, and Theatre on the Bounty* (Melbourne: Cambridge University Press, 1993).

Dening, Greg, *Readings/Writings* (Melbourne: Melbourne University Press, 1988).

Dick, Philip K., and Roger Zelazny, *Deus Irae* (London: Gollancz, 1977).

Dickinson, Peter, *The Weathermonger* (London: Gollancz, 1968)

Dickson, Gordon R., *The Dragon on the Border* (London: Grafton, 1993).

Dickson, Gordon R., *Time Storm* (New York: Baen: 1992).

Donaldson, Stephen, *The Chronicles of Thomas Covenant the Unbeliever* (London: HarperCollins, 1996).

Dubrow, Heather, *Genre* (London: Methuen, 1982).

Duby, Georges, *The Chivalrous Society* (Berkeley: University of California Press, 1977).

Duby, George, *Rural Economy and Country Life in the Medieval West*, tr. Cynthia Postan. (London: Edward Arnold, 1968).

Dunn, Wendy, *Dear Heart, How Like You This?* (Keene, NH: Metropolis Ink, 2002).

Eco, Umberto, *The Name of the Rose*, tr. William Weaver (London: Secker & Warburg, 1983).

Eco, Umberto, 'Towards a New Middle Ages', *On Signs*, ed. Marshall Blonsky (Baltimore, MD: The John Hopkins University Press, 1985).

Ellison R., Styron W., Penn Warren R. and Van Wooerd, 'The Uses of History in Fiction', *Southern Literary Journal* 1.2 (1969): 58–90.

Erskine, Barbara. *Lady of Hay* London: Joseph, 1986.

Farmer, Penelope. *Charlotte Sometimes*. London: The Bodley Head, 1985

Farmer, Philip Jose, *To Your Scattered Bodies Go* (London: Panther Books, 1985). *The Gate of Time*. London: Quartet Books, 1966

Feuchtwanger, Lion, 'The Purpose of the Historical Novel', tr. John Ahouse. Originally published as 'Vom Sinn des Historischen Romans', *Das Neue Tage-Buch*, 1935.

Feuchtwanger Memorial Library, <http://www.usc.edu/libraries/archives/arc/
libraries/feuchtwanger/writings/historical.html> accessed 23 December 2011

Finney, Jack, *Time and Again* (New York: Scribner, 1970).

Fleischman, Suzanne, *Tense and Narrativity: From Medieval Performance to Modern
Fiction* (Austin: University of Texas Press, 1990).

Flynn, Michael, *Eifelheim* (New York: Tor, 2006).

Ford, John M., *Dragon Waiting: A Masque of History* (New York: Timescape Books,
1983).

Fowles, John, *The French Lieutenant's Woman* (London: Panther, 1971).

Gabaldon, Diana, *Outlander* (New York: Delacorte Press, 2010).

Garcia y Robertson R. *Knight Errant*. New York: Forge, 2001.

Geertz, Clifford, *The Interpretation of Cultures: Selected Essays* (New York: Basic
Books, 1973).

Gesta Stephani, tr. K.L. Potter. (London: Nelson, 1955).

Given, James Buchanan, *Inquisition and Medieval Society: Power, Discipline, and
Resistance in Languedoc* (Ithaca, NY: Cornell University Press, 1997).

Godwin, Parke, *Sherwood* (New York: William Morrow, 1991).

Gomel, Elana, 'Shapes of the Past and the Future: Darwin and the Narratology of
Time Travel', *Narrative* 17.3 (2009), 334–52.

Goodrich, Peter, 'Magical Medievalism and the Fairy Tale in Susan Cooper's The
Dark is Rising Sequence', *The Lion and the Unicorn* 12.2 (1988), 165–77, <http://
muse.jhu.edu.virtual.anu.edu.au/journals/lion_and_the_unicorn> accessed 25
November 2015.

Gregory, Philippa, *The Other Boleyn Girl* (London: HarperCollins, 2001).

Gregory, Philippa, *The White Queen* (London: Simon & Schuster, 2009)

Grenville, Kate, *Searching for the Secret River* (Melbourne: The Text Publishing Company, 2006).

Griffiths, Tom, 'History and the creative imagination', *History Australia* 6.3 (2009),
74.1–74.16.

Guler, Kathleen Cunningham, *Into the Path of the Gods* (Steamboat Springs, CO:
Bardsong Press, 1998).

Harkness, Deborah, *Discovery of Witches* (London: Headline, 2011).

Harris, Stephen J. and Bryon L. Grigsby, eds, *Misconceptions about the Middle Ages*
(1999–2001), <http://the-orb.net/non_spec/missteps/misindex.html> accessed
3 October 2015.

Hartnett, Sonya, *The Children of the King* (London: Penguin/Viking, 2012).

Hatcher, John, 'Fiction as History: The Black Death and Beyond', *History* (2012), 3–23.

Hellekson, Karen, *The Alternate History: Refiguring Historical Time* (Kent, Ohio and
London: Kent State University Press, 2001).

Hellekson, Karen, 'Poul Anderson's Time Patrol as Anti-alternate History', *Extrapolation* 37.3 (1996), 234–44.

Herman, Paul, 'Performing History: How Historical Scholarship is Shaped by Epistemic Virtues', *History and Theory* 50 (2011), 1–19.

Heyer, Georgette, *Bath Tangle* (Bath: Paragon, 1955).

Heyer, Georgette, *Regency Buck* (London; Toronto: W. Heinemann, 1935).

Heyer, Georgette, *Simon the Coldheart* (London: Heinemann, 1978).

Heyer, Kent den, and Alexandra Fidyk, 'Configuring Historical Facts Through Historical Fiction: Agency, Art-In-Fact, and Imagination as Stepping Stones Between Then and Now', *Educational Theory* 57.2 (2007), 141–57.

Holbrook, David, *The Novel and Authenticity* (London and Totowa, NJ: Barnes & Noble, 1987).

Hollick, Helen, *A Hollow Crown: The Story of Emma, Queen of Saxon England* (London: William Heinemann, 2004).

Holmes, Frederick Michael, *The Historical Imagination: Postmodernism and the Treatment of the Past in Contemporary British Fiction* (Victoria, BC: University of Victoria, 1997).

Holton, R. *Jarring Witnesses, Modern Fiction and the Representation of History* (Hemel Hempstead: Harvester Wheatsheaf, 1994).

Hopkinson, Nalo, and Connie Willis, 'Science Fiction', <http://web.mit.edu/m-i-t/science_fiction/> accessed 1 October 2015.

Howell, Martha C., and Walter Prevenier, *From Reliable Sources: An Introduction to Historical Methods* (Ithaca, NY: Cornell University Press, 2001).

Hühn, Peter et al., eds, *The Living Handbook of Narratology* (Hamburg: Hamburg University, <http://www.lhn.uni-hamburg.de/> accessed 23 Aug 2015.

Hume, Kathryn, 'Medieval Romance and Science Fiction: The Anatomy of a Resemblance', *Journal of Popular Culture* 16.1 (1982), 15–26.

Hutcheon, Linda, *A Poetics of Postmodernism: History, Theory, Fiction* (New York: Routledge, 1988).

Jacobs, Naomi, *The Character of Truth: Historical Figures in Contemporary Fiction* (Carbondale: Southern Illinois University Press, 1990).

Jaeger, Stephan, 'Poietic Worlds and Experientiality in Historiographic Narrative', *SPIEL* 30 (2011) 1, 29–50.

James, Edward, and Farah Mendlesohn, eds, *The Cambridge Companion to Science Fiction* (Cambridge: Cambridge University Press, 2003).

Jeffries, Mike, *Hidden Echoes* (London: HarperCollins, 1993).

Jenkins, Keith, Sue Morgan and Alun Munslow, *Manifestos for History* (London and New York: Routledge, 2007).

Kay, Guy Gavriel, *A Song for Arbonne* (London: Harper Collins, 1992).

Kay, Guy Gavriel, *Tigana* (New York: Roc, 1990).

Kinsella, John, *Genre* (Fremantle, WA: Fremantle Arts Centre Press, 1997).

Knight, Stephen, *Robin Hood: A Mythic Biography* (Ithaca, NY: Cornell University Press, 2003).

Kushner, Ellen, *Thomas the Rhymer: A Ballad of Elfland* (London: VGSF, 1992).

LaCapra, Dominick, *History, Politics, and the Novel* (Ithaca, NY: Cornell University Press, 1987).

Larbalestier, Justine, *The Battle of the Sexes in Science Fiction* (Lebanon, NH: Wesleyan 2002).

le Roy Ladurie, E., *Montaillou, Catholics and Cathars in a French Village, 1294–324*, tr. B. Bray (Harmondsworth: Penguin, 1981).

Leiber, Fritz, *Changewar* (New York: Ace Science Fiction, 1983).

Levin A.E., 'English-Language SF as a Socio-Cultural Phenomenon', tr. Yuri Prizel, *Science Fiction Studies* 13.4, Pt 3 (November 1977), <http://www.depauw.edu/sfs/backissues/13/levin13.htm> accessed 10 December 2014.

Lewis, C.S., *That Hideous Strength: A Modern Fairy Tale for Grown-ups* (London: Bodley Head, 1945).

Lindenberger, H., *The History in Literature: On Value, Genre, Institutions* (New York: Columbia University Press, 1990).

Lowenthal, David, *The Past is a Foreign Country* (Cambridge: Cambridge University Press, 1985).

Luckett, Dave, *A Dark Winter* (Norwood, SA: Omnibus Books, 1998).

Luckett, Dave, *Subversive Activity* (Fremantle, WA: VIVID Publishing, 2009).

Lukács, Georg, *The Historical Novel*, tr. Hanna and Stanley Michel. (London: Merlin Press, 1962).

Lukács, Georg, *The Theory of the Novel*. tr. Anna Bostock. (Cambridge, Mass: The MIT Press, 1971).

McAuley, Paul J., *Pasquale's Angel* (London: Gollancz, 1995).

MacAvoy R. A. *The Book of Kells*. Toronto, Bantam Books, 1985.

McDonald, Ian. *Brasyl*. London: Gollancz, 2007

McGill, Allan, *Historical Knowledge, Historical Error: A Contemporary Guide to Practice* (Chicago and London: The University of Chicago Press, 2007).

McKenna, Mark, 'Writing the Past: History, Literature and the Public Sphere in Australia'. Public lecture delivered 1 December 2005, Queensland College of Art, Brisbane, <http://www.humanitieswritingproject.net.au/McKenna.pdf> accessed 10 March 2006.

MacKeod, Anne Scott, 'Writing Backward: Modern Models in Historical Fiction', *The Horn Book Magazine* (January/February1998), <http://www.hbook.com/magazine/articles/1998/jan98_macleod.asp> accessed 3 July 2013.

McMullen, Sean, *The Time Engine* (New York: Tor, 2008).

Magistra et Mater, 'Why I no Longer Read Historical Fiction', <http://magistraet-mater.blog.co.uk/2009/08/10/why-i-no-longer-read-historical-fiction-i-read-a-6693060/> accessed 27 October 2015.

Maitland, Karen, *Company of Liars: A Novel of the Plague* (London: Michael Joseph, 2008).

Malvasi, Mark G., and Nelson Jeffrey, eds, *Remembered Past: John Lukacs on History, Historians and Historical Knowledge. A Reader* (Wilmington, DE: ISI Books, 2005).

Mantel, Hilary, *Wolf Hall* (London: Fourth Estate, 2009).

Martin, George R. R., *A Game of Thrones* (London: HarperVoyager, 1998).

Martyn, Isolde, *The Lady and the Unicorn* (Sydney: Transworld Bantam, 1998).

Masson, Sophie, *Moonlight & Ashes* (North Sydney: Random House, 2012).

Masson, Sophie, *Scarlet in the Snow* (North Sydney: Random House, 2013).

Mayne, William. *Earthfasts*. Hodder London: Children's Books, 1995.

Mendlesohn, Farah. *Rhetorics of Fantasy* (Middletown, CT: Wesleyan University Press, 2008).

Miller, J.H., 'Narrative and History', *Journal of English Literary History* 41 (1974), 455–73.

Miller, Walter M., Jr., *A Canticle for Leibowitz* (London: Orbit, 1990).

Mink, L.O., 'History and Fiction as Modes of Comprehension', *New Literary History* 1 (1970), 541–58.

Moorcock, Michael, *Behold the Man* (London: Allison and Busby, 1969).

Moorcock, Michael, *Dancers at the End of Time* (London: Gollancz, 1993).

Moorcock, Michael, *Nomad of the Time Streams: A Scientific Romance* (London: Orion, 1996).

Mortimer, Ian, *The Time Traveller's Guide to Medieval England: A Handbook for Visitors to the Fourteenth Century* (London: Bodley Head, 2008).

Moses, A. Dirk, 'The Public Relevance of Historical Studies: A Rejoinder to Hayden White', Forum: The Public Role of History 3. *History and Theory* 44 (2005), 339–47.

Munslow, Alun, *The Future of History* (Basingstoke, Hampshire; New York: Palgrave Macmillan, 2010).

Munslow, Alun, 'The Historian as Author', *SPIEL* 30 (2011), 73–88.

Nitz, Julia, 'In Fact No Fiction: Historiographical Paratext', *SPIEL* 30.1 (2011), 89–111.

Onega, Susana ed., *Telling Histories: Narrativizing History, Historicizing Literature* (Amsterdam: Rodopi, 1995).

Park, Ruth. *Playing Beatie Bow*. Ringwood: Puffin, 1980.

Pavel, T., 'Literary Genres or Norms and Good Habits', *New Literary History: a Journal of Theory and Interpretation* 34.2 (2003), 201–10.

Penman, Sharon Kay, *When Christ and His Saints Slept* (New York: Ballantine Books, 1995).

Pevel, Pierre, *The Alchemist in the Shadows*, tr. Thomas Clegg (Amherst, NY: Pyr, 2011).

Phelan, James, *Reading People, Reading Plots: Character, Progression, and the Interpretation of Narrative* (Chicago: University of Chicago Press, 1989).

Phillips, M.S., 'Histories, Micro and Literary: Problems of Genre and Distance', *New Literary History* 34.2 (2003), 211–29.

Piper, H. Beam, *Fuzzy Sapiens* (New York: Ace Books, 1964).

Polack, Gillian, 'Chatting with Sharon Kay Penman and Elizabeth Chadwick', *Bibliobuffet* (4 July 2011), <http://www.bibliobuffet.com/bookish-dreaming/1546-chatting-with-sharon-kay-penman-and-elizabeth-chadwick-070311> accessed 6 July 2011.

Polack, Gillian, 'Conceptualising the Past: How Fiction Writers Talk About The Middle Ages', *Sheffield Hallam Working Papers on the Web, v. 9 Dec.: Historicising the Historical Novel*, <http://extra.shu.ac.uk/wpw/historicising/Polack. htm> accessed 21 June 2006

Polack, Gillian, 'Horrible Historians', *Subterranean Magazine* 4 (2008): 26–30.

Polack, Gillian, 'How Fiction Writers Use the Middle Ages', *AntiTHESIS*, <http://www.english.unimelb.edu.au/antithesis/forum-3/09-GillianPolack.html> accessed 21 June 2006

Polack, Gillian, *Illuminations* (Lake Charles, LA: Trivium Publishing, 2003).

Polack, Gillian, 'Margo Lanagan interviewed by Gillian Polack (Australia)' *Europa* (2014), <http://scifiportal.eu/margo-lanagan/> accessed 1 October 2015

Polack, Gillian, 'More from think.com' *Even in A Little Thing* (2005), <http://gill-polack.livejournal.com/33014.html> accessed 10 September 2014.

Polack, Gillian, 'Novelists and their History', in *Rethinking History: The Journal of Theory and Practice* 18.4 (2014), 522–42.

Polack, Gillian, and Katrin Kania, *The Middle Ages Unlocked* (Stroud: Amberley Publishing, 2015).

Pollington, S., *Leechcraft. Early English Charms, Plant-Lore and Healing* (Little Downham, Ely: Anglo-Saxon Books, 2000).

Prestwich, Michael, *The Three Edwards: War and State in England 1272–377* (London: Routledge, 2004).

Pulman, Felicity, *Ghost Boy* (Sydney: Random House, 2004).

Pulman, Felicity, *I, Morgana* (Sydney: Momentum, 2014).

Pulman, Felicity, *A Ring Through Time* (Sydney: HarperCollins, 2013).

Pulman, Felicity, *Rosemary for Remembrance* (Sydney: Random House, 2005).

Rabkin, Eric S., 'Atavism and Utopia', *No Place Else: Explorations in Utopian and Dystopian Fiction*, eds Eric S. Rabkin, Martin H. Greenberg and Joseph D. Olander (Carbondale, IL: Southern Illinois University Press, 1983), 1–10.

Rainbolt, William, 'He Disagreed with the History, But He Liked the Story', *Writing History/Writing Fiction: A Virtual Conference Session*, <http://www.albany.edu/history/hist_fict/Rainbolt/Rainboltes.htm> accessed 5 July 2009.

Reynolds, Susan, *Fiefs and Vassals. The Medieval Evidence Reinterpreted* (Oxford: Clarendon, 1994).

Riffaterre, M., *Fictional Truth* (Baltimore, MD: The Johns Hopkins University Press, 1990).

Rigney, Ann, 'All This Happened, More or Less: What a Novelist Made of the Bombing of Dresden', *History and Theory* 47 (2009), 5–24.

Robertson, Fiona, *Legitimate histories: Scott, Gothic, and the Authorities of Fiction* (Oxford: Clarendon Press, 1994).

Robinson, Kim Stanley, *Galileo's Dream* (London: HarperVoyager, 2009).

Rogerson, J.W., 'Slippery Words: Myth', *Sacred Narrative: Readings in the Theory of Myth*, ed. Alan Dundes (Berkeley: University of California Press, 1984), 62–71.

Rose, Mark, *Alien Encounters: Anatomy of Science Fiction* (New York: toExcel, 1981).

Russ, Joanna, *Extra(ordinary) People* (London: The Women's Press S. F., 1985).

Sachs, Aaron, 'Letters to a Tenured Historian: Imagining History as Creative Nonfiction – or Maybe Even Poetry', *Rethinking History: The Journal of Theory and Practice* 14: 1 (n.d.), 5–38.

Samuelson, David N., 'Modes of Extrapolation: The Formulas of Hard SF', *Science-Fiction Studies* 20 (1993), 191–232.

Sandison, Alan, and Robert Dingley eds, *Histories of the Future: Studies in Fact, Fantasy and Science Fiction* (New York: Palgrave, 2000).

Scott, Joan W., 'Fantasy Echo: History and the Construction of Identity', *Critical Inquiry* 27, 2 (2001), 284–304.

Scott, Joan, 'Forum: Holberg Prize Symposium Doing Decentered History 2. Storytelling', *History and Theory* 50 (2011), 203–9.

Seed, David, *Science Fiction: A Very Short Introduction* (Oxford: Oxford University Press, 2011).

Seitel, Peter, 'Theorizing Genres: Interpreting Works', *New Literary History*, Theorizing Genres I 34. 2 (2003), 275–97.

Sharratt, Mary, *Daughters of the Witching Hill* (Chicago: Houghton Mifflin Harcourt, 2010).

Shaw, Bob, *The Two-Timers* (London: Gollancz SF, 1969).

Silverberg, Robert, *Up the Line* (London: VGSF, 1987).

Simmons, Dan, *Hyperion* (London: Headline Book Publishing, 1989).

Southgate, Beverley, *History Meets Fiction* (London: Pearson Educational, 2009).

Stableford, Brian, *The Walking Shadow* (Glasgow: Fontana, 1979).

Stewart, Mary, *The Crystal Cave* (London: World Books, 1971).

Strohm, Paul, 'History without historicism?', *Postmedieval: A Journal of Medieval Cultural Studies* 1 (2010), 380–91.

Taglia, Kathryn. 'The Cultural Construction of Childhood: Baptism, Communion and Confirmation', *Women, Marriage and Family in Medieval Christendom*, eds Constance M. Rousseau and Joel T. Rosenthal (Kalamazoo, MI: Western Michigan University, 1998), 255–88.

Tarr, Judith, *The Isle of Glass* (New York: Orb Books, 1993).

Teo, Hsu-Ming, 'Historical Fictions and Fictions of History', *Rethinking History*, 15.2 (2011), 297.

Tey, Josephine, *The Daughter of Time* (London: Peter Davies, 1951)

Thomas, Keith, *History and Literature* (Swansea: University College of Swansea, 1988).

Thompson, Raymond H., *Taliesin's Successors: Interviews with Authors of Modern Arthurian Literature* (Rochester, NY: The Camelot Project, 1999), <http://d.lib.rochester.edu/camelot/text/thompson-taliesins-successors> accessed 25 November 2015.

Tolkien, J. R. R., *Lord of the Rings*, 2nd edn (New York: Ballantine, 1973).

Tolkien, J. R. R., 'On Fairy Tales', *The Monster and the Critics and Other Essays*, ed. Christopher Tolkien (Boston: Houghton Mifflin, 1984).

Tosh, John, 'In defence of applied history: The History and Policy website', <http://www.historyandpolicy.org/papers/policy-paper-37.html> accessed 1 June 2009

Tosh, John, *Why History Matters* (Basingstoke, Hampshire: Palgrave Macmillan, 2008).

Tosh, John, with Sean Lang, *The Pursuit of History: Aims, Methods and New Directions in the Study of Modern History*, 4th edn (Harlow: Longman Educational, 2006).

Treece, Henry, *The Children's Crusade* (Harmondsworth: Puffin, 1964).

Trigg, Stephanie, 'Medievalism and Convergence Culture: Researching the Middle Ages for Fiction and Film', *Parergon* 25.2 (2008), 99–118.

Turner, J.W., 'The Kinds of Historical Fiction: An Essay in Definition and Methodology', *Genre* 12 (1979), 333–55.

Turtledove, Harry, *The Guns of the South: A Novel of the Civil War* (New York: Ballantine Books, 1992).

Twain, Mark, *A Connecticut Yankee in King Arthur's Court* (New York: Charles L. Webster and Co., 1889).

Uttley, Alison, *A Traveller in Time* (London: Puffin Books, 1977).

Vallar, Cindy, 'Historical Fiction vs History', <http://www.cindyvallar.com/histfic.html> accessed 3 April 2005

Van Woodward, C., 'The Uses of History in Fiction', *The Southern Literary Journal* 1 (1969), 57–90.

Vidal, Gore, *Live From Golgotha* (London: Abacus, 1992).

Vivanco, Laura, 'History and 'Wallpaper' History', *Teach Me Tonight: Musings on Romance Fiction from an Academic Perspective*, 3 July 2006, <http://teachme-tonight.blogspot.com/2006/07/history-and-wallpaper-history.html> accessed 22 June 2010.

Vonnegut, Kurt, *Slaughterhouse-Five* (London: Jonathan Cape, 1970).

Wainwright, Brian, *Within the Fetterlock* (Lake Charles, LA: Trivium Publishing, 2004).

Waldrop, Howard, *Them Bones* (New York: Ace, 1984).

Weinstein, M.A., 'The Creative Imagination in Fiction and History', *Genre* 9 (1976), 263–77.

Westerfeld, Scott, *Leviathan* (Camberwell: Penguin, 2009).

White, Hayden, *The Content of Form: Narrative Discourse and Historical Representation* (Baltimore, MD: The Johns Hopkins University Press, 1987).

White, Hayden, *The Fiction of Narrative: Essays on History, Literature, and Theory, 1957–2007* (Baltimore, MD: The Johns Hopkins University Press, 2010).

White, Hayden, *Figural Realism: Studies in the Mimesis Effect* (Baltimore, MD: The Johns Hopkins University Press, 1999).

White, Hayden, *Metahistory: The Historical Imagination in Nineteenth-Century Europe* (Baltimore. MD: John Hopkins University Press, 1973).

White, T.H., *The Once and Future King* (London: HarperCollins, 1996).

Willis, Connie, *Blackout* (New York: Spectra Ballantine Books, 2010).

Willis, Connie, *Doomsday Book* (New York: Bantam, 1994).

Willis, Connie, Interview with Nick Gevers, Infinity Plus website. Originally published in *Interzone* (November 2001), <http://www.infinityplus.co.uk/nonfiction/intcwillis.htm> accessed 4 June 2005

Willis, Connie, *To Say Nothing of the Dog: How We found the Bishop's Bird Stump at Last* (New York: Bantam Spectra, 1998).

Wolfe, Gene, *The Devil in a Forest* (London: Panther, 1985).

Womack, Jack, *Terraplane* (London: Unwin, 1989).

Woodiwiss, Kathleen E., *Forever in Your Embrace* (London: Piatkus, 1992).

Woodiwiss, Kathleen E., *Shanna* (London: HarperCollins e-book, 2009).

Worth, Sandra, *The Rose of York: Love and War* (Yarnel, AZ: End Table Books, 2003).

Wrede Patricia C., 'Fantasy Worldbuilding Questions', <https://www.sfwa.org/2009/08/fantasy-worldbuilding-questions/> accessed 10 October 2015.

Writing History/Writing Fiction: A Virtual Conference, <http://www.albany.edu/history/hist_fict/home.htm> accessed 6 April 2011.

Wroe, Ann, *A Fool and his Money: Life in a Partitioned Town in Fourteenth-Century France* (New York: Hill and Wang, 1995).

Wyndham, John, *The Seeds of Time* (London: Joseph, 1956).

Yaszek, Lisa, 'Cultural History', *Routledge Companion to Science Fiction*, eds Mark Bould, Andrew M. Butler, Adam Roberts and Sherryl Vint (New York and Oxford: Routledge, 2009): 194–203.

Zornado, Joseph, 'A Poetics of History: Karen Cushman's Medieval World', *The Lion and the Unicorn* 21.2 (1997), 251–66.

Index

CPSIA information can be obtained
at www.ICGtesting.com
Printed in the USA
LVHW050852120121
676265LV00006B/396